THE BOOK OF
SAMSON

A watercolour painting of SAMSON, *by railway artist, Jonathan Clay.*

THE BOOK OF
SAMSON

*The life and work of a
lead mining locomotive…*

By Paul Jarman

RCL Publications

THE BOOK OF SAMSON
First Edition
© Author & RCL Publications, June 2016

ISBN
978-0-9565157-5-9

Published by
RCL PUBLICATIONS
*Cambrian Forge, Garndolbenmaen,
Gwynedd, LL51 9RX*

*Printed by
Lavenham Press,
47 Water Street, Lavenham
Suffolk, CO10 9RN*

CONTENTS

ACKNOWLEDGEMENTS & NOTES VI
PREFACE VII
INTRODUCTION VIII

CHAPTER 1   *The London Lead Company and the Cornish Hush Tramway* 1

CHAPTER 2   *The Route of the Tramway* 7

CHAPTER 3   *Stephen Lewin and the Poole Foundry – the first* SAMSON 20

CHAPTER 4   SAMSON *in Victorian narrow gauge locomotive design context* . . . 28

CHAPTER 5   *Narrow gauge steam locomotives
in the Durham dales lead mining industry* 36

CHAPTER 6   SAMSON *reborn* 44

CHAPTER 7   *Construction in detail – frames and footplate* 51

CHAPTER 8   *Construction in detail – the engine unit* 65

CHAPTER 9   *Construction in detail – the boiler* 82

CHAPTER 10   SAMSON *into service* 94

CHAPTER 11   *The project scope broadens* 112

CHAPTER 12   *What remains of the other tramways?* 119

APPENDICES
1. The Story of a Determined Man – a short autobiography by David Young XI
2. Where does the inspiration come from? XII
3. SAMSON *and the modern Safety Management System* XIV
4. A Thorny Question: What Colour was SAMSON? XIV
5. Where did the name come from? XV
6. Main technical details XVI
5. Boiler components XVII

REFERENCES & BIBLIOGRAPHY XVIII
THE BEAMISH CONNECTION XIX
INDEX XXI

ACKNOWLEDGEMENTS

I am sure that when any author sits down to pen the acknowledgments, they are acutely conscious of leaving out a vital name or contributor. It is therefore with great care and not a little apprehension that I set out the most considered paragraph in this book! If there is anyone that I have forgotten to mention by name, it is not through neglect of their role in this story, just an omission caused by the inevitable diversity of roles played in the creation of even a very small steam locomotive.

It is also worth according a great degree of gratitude to the authors Russell Wear and Eric Lees, who in 1978 co-authored their book on the subject of Stephen Lewin and the Poole Foundry (with that title), published jointly by the Industrial Railway and Industrial Locomotive Societies. Whilst articles have appeared on the subject of Stephen Lewin (or more accurately, some of the locomotives built by the company), the work of Messrs Wear and Lees still stands as the definitive account of the often troubled company and its products. Their book, and the sources which they were able to identify, are instrumental in ensuring the construction of the replica Samson was feasible, whilst creating an interest in the subject and company that went much further than simply another steam locomotive from the 1870s...

The numerous contributors to the construction of SAMSON and supporters of the project (and the production of this book)
included: Chris Armstrong, Duncan Ballard, Matt Beddard, Mike Boase, Bryan and Dorothy Chambers, Gerry Clarke, Matt Ellis, Bob Garnett, Dave Grindley, Graham Hood, Dave Howell, Graham Lee, Andy Martin, Dave McGeorge, Alan Moore, Graham Morris, Alan Nicholson, Andrew Neale, Matthew Plowman, Terry Powell, Jim Rees, Mark Smithers, Ken Swan, Tony Vollans, James Waterfield, Julie Wilson, Andy Wright and David Young.

I would also like to thank Roy Link for his beautiful design work on this book and for publishing it as part of his admired and much sought after range of titles.

All photographs featured are from the Beamish Museum collection, unless otherwise stated, or have been taken by David Young or the author.

Finally, I should like to mention two long-suffering wives! Maureen Young must have wondered what had possessed her husband as he ratcheted up 40+ hour weeks in the near obsessive pursuit of Samson, delighting him with her approval of the finished locomotive! Sarah Jarman has been a great support to me, both during the project (and so many other projects!) in one role and also in the writing of this book as author – the drumming keys of the keyboard late in the night never once upsetting her very forgiving temperament!

Paul Jarman

NOTES

For those unfamiliar with imperial measurements and pre-decimal money the following comparisons are given.

		1 ton	–	1.01 tonnes
1 inch	–	25.43 millimetres	¼d = 1 farthing (d)	–	0.104 pence (p)
12 inches = 1 foot	–	0.304 metres	1 old penny (d)	–	0.416 pence (p)
3 feet = 1 yard	–	0.9144 metres	12 pennies = 1 shilling (s)	–	5 pence (p)
22 yards = 1 chain	–	20.11 metres	2 shillings (s)	–	10 pence (p)
1760 yards = 1 mile	–	1.60 kilometres	5 shillings (s)	–	25 pence (p)
1 cubic yard	–	0.765 cubic metres	10 shillings (s)	–	50 pence (p)
1 acre	–	0.40 hectares	240 pennies = 1 pound (£)	–	1 pound (£)
1 gallon	–	4.536 litres	21 shillings = 1 guinea	–	1 pound and 5 pence

PREFACE

THIS BOOK, WHILST FOCUSED on the creation of Beamish Museum's new-build replica of an 1874-built railway locomotive, is also a story of the motivations and passions of those people who have a weakness for the earlier industrial steam locomotive designs, whether they survive or were consigned to history. As a result the narrative covers the wider story of how the new SAMSON came to be built and the incredible work of a Museum volunteer called David Young whose drive and energy in the advanced years of his retirement are an example, encouragement and inspiration to all of those who have had the great pleasure to witness his formidable work ethic in action.

The author on the footplate of Coffee Pot No.1 of 1871.

The result of this has been a series of fascinating, fully operational, steam engines that Beamish Museum can demonstrate to its visitors, where they can observe and engage with engines ranging in date from 1871 to 2016 – no mean feat! Readers may also wonder if this book marks the end of the story? As this book is being written, a stationary engine of single cylinder type and originating in an historically obscure local foundry is under restoration to full working order at Beamish, by David, where it will once again fulfil the role its creators originally intended.

It is therefore with great pleasure that this modest publication is dedicated to David Young and his ever-supportive wife Maureen, and seeks to place on record both his contribution to the Museum at Beamish and also put in print the journey taken in creating a brand new steam locomotive based on one which survived only in the form of one photograph, two engravings and a contemporary description from the leading trade magazines of its day.

Paul Jarman, February 2016

INTRODUCTION

Above: This is the photograph that started it all, in many ways it is the only tangible proof that we still have of SAMSON's existence beyond the marketing literature of its manufacturer. A number of prints of the original glass negative appear to have survived, including this one from the Beamish archive. It is interesting that in some reproductions, detail changes are evident. The most notable is that some views show a hole in the flywheel, through which the regulator rod can be glimpsed. It may therefore be the case that some prints have been touched up, whilst others are under exposed. The photographer's identity remains unknown, and surely this was not the only plate that he exposed that day? Perhaps the appearance of this book will unearth further images taken on this occasion, but for now it is all we have…

NE CAN ONLY IMAGINE WHAT the group of tough, hardened lead miners made of SAMSON as they were marshalled into a line in order to pose for a photographer's camera. Their relentless toil, written into every line of their faces, had caused scant excitement in the outside world over their many years at work, or the years of their fathers and grandfathers. Yet here they were now, asked to provide a backdrop to a novelty, a 'phase', a steam locomotive of such diminutive stature that it stood barely able to hold its own presence against the horses it had been brought in to replace.

Faces set, the image was captured by the unknown photographer, surely not the only image captured that day, but the only one which we know to have survived and one which has been of colossal fascination to a small number of people in the four decades since it was brought to a wider audience in the book *Stephen Lewin and the Poole Foundry*. Yet, it takes only a few men to gaze upon such a scene and wonder what the subject must have been like before it was reduced to a footnote in history at the turn of the last century; living on only with a single photograph to prove it ever existed whilst those who were pressed to stand sentry-like behind this engine, known as SAMSON (some say SAMPSON), have been all but forgotten, likely as not even by their own descendants.

In our affluent society, richer than ever before and with leisure time a luxury those men in the photograph could only have dreamt about, those gazing upon such an image can, if the mood takes them, set about recreating what they behold. So it is that the heritage movement can cast off the technicality of extinct history and rebuild it, whether in architecture, as sailing vessels, lost pre-industrial technology and, so important to us in this story, as a steam locomotive. Not even a surviving strand of DNA is required, for the imaginations that created the actors within the historical narrative can be imagined anew, and so the 'Everest' of lost locomotives can be conquered, as we have seen with the recreation of so many 'new-builds' both completed or under construction in our present century.

Where does the motivation to recreate what has been lost to us come from? Particularly as, in the case of the steam locomotive, so many deserving cases lie silent in sidings across the land? Perhaps it is the desire not just to see the steam locomotive alive, but the compulsion to walk the path of its creator, to face the same challenges and gain some insight into the mind of someone unknown to us and very certainly long-departed from this earth.

Maybe it is the desire to do something others are not, nor would likely be to do? Or maybe it is simply the appeal of a subject that otherwise cannot be accessed by the majority of our senses in any way other than by its detailed recreation in three dimensional form? The motivations are no doubt as varied as those who turn a curiosity into tangibility, but for myself and David Young, the principal 'maker' (to use a term contemporary with the source material), the attraction to that single photograph taken in the 1870s and revealing the original SAMSON in all of its fascinating detail was irresistible, and so set us on a journey that built upon the paths we had trodden before in our pursuit of the *unappreciated* (my emphasis) Victorian industrial steam locomotive.

Thus it was that, with the project to build a new SAMSON for Beamish Museum concluded, I sat down to write the story of this 'new' SAMSON. It quickly became clear that a degree of context, both historical in regard to the original SAMSON, and as a rationale for what motivated this project and how we came to it, was going to be core to the narrative. It is therefore my earnest hope that this book will be regarded in the broadest terms, not just as a record of one particular steam locomotive's construction, but as a means of illuminating the role of people within such an undertaking.

In doing so it may perhaps have some small appeal to those not infected with the wonderful enthusiasm for steam locomotives that we enjoy, and might pass muster with those interested in understanding what makes people do what they do. Inevitably there is a danger of creating a book of such limited appeal that we shall sell but a few copies, but as a record of 'our' SAMSON's inception and construction, a locomotive we hope will endure for very many generations, then it will serve as an instructive record of that process for others who may be as curious about this SAMSON as we were about the original.

CHAPTER 1
THE LONDON LEAD COMPANY AND THE CORNISH HUSH TRAMWAY

This undated view of the staff of the London Lead Company workshops at Middleton-in-Teesdale appears to show a young Mark Pinkey on the front row, left hand side. Also of note are the bottom-discharge lead mine tubs (a reconstruction of which now acts as a tender for the new Samson) and also the spare wheelsets. The staff appears to be quite a sizable one, attending to every need of the estate and the mining operations across the company concessions in this part of the county.

HE MODERN MOTORIST, scrambling their way across Middleton Common on the sinuous route that now forms the B6278 from Middleton-in-Teesdale to Stanhope over the roof of the North Pennines, will almost certainly be unaware that as they begin the long descent from the summit at White Hill (1609 feet above sea level) they can gaze north eastwards upon almost the entire route of the Cornish Hush Tramway as it hugs the western slope of Nookerley Hill. Drivers daring to glance away from the tarmac winding before them and fix their eyes across the heather and moor of the common might briefly discern the tramway as it follows the vegetation change along the hillside in the distance, following the path of the Howden Burn towards the Bollihope Burn at Whitfield Brow.

They may even detect the spoil heaps, risen out of years of lead and fluorspar extraction in the area, but they are unlikely to realise that the healing scar of the tramway's route, of not much less than one mile in length, was once home to a little steam locomotive and that for a very short period of time, such a view might have revealed this engine bustling along the tramway with lead ore for the crusher at Whitfield Brow and empty waggons returning to the mine at Cornish Hush.

On a sunny 29 August 1891 a smaller team gather for their photograph to be taken at the workshops in Middleton-in-Teesdale. Mark Pinkney, by now 71 years of age, sits at the front of the group. The smaller number of staff no doubt reflects the diminishing scale of the company's activities, which would eventually cease altogether in 1905 when the company was wound up. Even by the time this photograph was taken many of the mineral rights had been surrendered, including Cornish Hush in 1883. It raises a tantalising question – was SAMSON (which we know was almost certainly removed, for scrap, from Middleton-in-Teesdale in 1904) stored at the works at this date, possibly providing power for machinery on site?

The London Lead Company was owned by Quaker industrialists and prospered over a lengthy period from 1692 until 1905, though the latter part of its life from 1882 was considered its declining era, up to the point at which it was wound up. Perhaps of most interest to the story of SAMSON is the period from 1790 top 1882 when, as described by Arthur Rastrick in his book 'Two centuries of Industrial Welfare – The London (Quaker) Lead Company 1692 – 1905', the company consolidated its national interests in the north Pennines, primarily between the rivers Tyne and Swale.

The company had a reputation as a paternal employer, true to the Quaker traditions enshrined within its owner's characters and resulting in exercises in village construction, developing schools and providing subsidised food and medical welfare for its workers. Over two centuries the company ensured its strong foothold and

economic resilience through careful management and maintaining a competitive edge by investment and technological advancement. It is this backdrop that perhaps best illuminates the mechanism by which a steam locomotive was introduced to a very small part of the company's portfolio as it sought the latest in engineering progress. Recognising the harsh country and difficult terrain in which the mines of the Pennine hills were located, the London Lead Company promoted and made grants towards the creation of new roads or the improvement of existing routes. This also included bridges, such a vital part of the transport infrastructure.

The arrival of railways into the region opened up new transport routes for the company, a trend reflected in the arrival of the Stockton & Darlington Railway, promoted by Edward Pease a well-known Darlington Quaker and businessman. The company was

A fine but undated portrait of Mark Pinkney in his later years, found in the photographic archive at Beamish and an image that takes on so much more when the subject's life and contribution is known, at least in part.

ever alert to the opportunities new railway lines would create for the development of the business. The technology of railways in mining had also been explored, with iron rails being used underground on the drawing levels, this usage extending in 1817 to encompass the surface sidings and routes, including those like the 1 ft 10 in gauge Cornish Hush Tramway, maximising the benefits of horse operation on these waggon ways.

By the early 1890s the company was suffering from increasing competition and, perhaps recognising the increasing age of the members of its governing body, began to consider its future. This resulted in it divesting itself of its operations, the end being decided in 1902 and finally coming in 1905 when the remaining leases were sold to the Vielle Montagne Company, who continued to mine zinc in some areas until the Second World War.

Cornish Hush, so named after the men from Cornwall who first worked out the veins crossing the Howden Burn, was both hushed (see Chapter 3) and also worked by shafts and levels. Lead ore (Galena) occurs in vertical veins which were exposed by creating water reservoirs which would then be released to scour channels across the hillside, removing everything from the sub-soil upwards. Later, the London Lead Company developed the mine and from 1868 to its closure, the rather disappointing volume of 6483 tons

of lead ore were extracted and transferred, via the 1ft 10in gauge tramway, to Whitfield Brow for processing in the works there. This was considered a poor return on the investment.

In August 1970, after seven decades of disuse, the mine was reopened by Swiss Aluminium Mining (UK) Ltd (abbreviated to SAMUK) in order for them to prospect for fluorspar. In connection with this another narrow gauge railway was built, this time to 2ft gauge, a Greenwood & Batley 'Greenbat' battery electric locomotive being provided new in 1971 (later removed to another SAMUK site in 1975). The railway ran underground, with the mine entrance of the Horse Level being rebuilt and given a stone arch entrance and doors for security. The locomotive certainly ran underground, something that SAMSON is assumed not to have done given the danger of fumes from the engine underground (even in a non-gassy environment).

The fluorspar operation was road-served, with several buildings of recognisable 1970s ancestry being erected to support the operation, including a laboratory, locomotive garage and workshops. Following abandonment of the scheme in 1975, the site became derelict, with the buildings later being demolished and removed. The locomotive, GB 420288, was removed to Cambokeels Mine in 1975, returning to be used on site clearance and tracklifting before moving on to Stanhopeburn Mine in May 1977. It returned to Cambokeels and was seen there in February 1978. Shortly after it moved again, being seen at Yew Tree mine at Bollihope in October 1978. It was then sold to Honister Mine in Cumbria, by August 1983 and was then scrapped, date unknown.

Turning back to the 1870s once again, 'that' photograph compels further detailed study. The anonymity of the photographer has already been mentioned, but the identity of one person depicted is known, this being Mr Mark Pinkney. He appears fourth from the right, hands on hips and pipe in mouth. This stance exudes a presence that suggests that he was in charge, as well it might, because he was! Mark Pinkney was the Chief Engineer for the London Lead Company, based out of their Hude Top Fitting Shops, covering all mining and estate activity, at Middleton-in-Teesdale. Mark Pinkney was born on the 7 January 1820 in Middleton-in-Teesdale, County Durham. In 1841 he married Sarah Bowman, also born in 1820, and they eventually had nine children, one of whom, Mrs (Sarah-Ann or Mary) Hutchinson, he latterly lived with in Market Place, Middleton-in-Teesdale. He was widowed in 1894 and went on to achieve a grand age of 85, dying on the 26 May 1905. His obituary, in the Teesdale Mercury, read:

'Mr Pinkney was head engineer of the London Lead Company, at Hude Top Fitting Shops, for a very large number of years, a position he very ably filled. Mr Pinkney was also an angler of no small merit, and although considerably over 80 years of age he followed his hobby till quite recently. The Pinkney family are numerous in Teesdale, and a large number of them are descendants of old Mark.'

Above: In 1970 the mine was reopened by Swiss Aluminium UK in order to prospect for fluorspar. This early view, taken in 1971, shows the work to prepare the site underway. Later images of the operation show that the adit mouth was rebuilt and fitted with doors and that a substantial drystone retaining wall was constructed to the right of the mine entrance, here seen consisting of loose stone and waste. Narrow gauge Hudson 'Jubilee' track has been laid but there is no sign of the brand new battery electric locomotive.

The remains of the mine shop rear wall are apparent above the compressor, the holes for floor joists of the first floor being just visible. This would be the building which appears on the extreme left of the 1870s photograph of SAMSON, *the locomotive being stood around about where the base of an inverted 'U' skip body can be seen in this view.*

Right: A selection of Hudson tubs and an air compressor decorate the scene outside the adit mouth. The area between the compressor and the entrance to the mine would subsequently have a substantial dry stone wall constructed alongside the track.

Photos: Peter Jackson

Phot: Peter Jackson

Phot: ebgb – Adit Now Forum

Above: An overall view of the site, showing the siding disappearing into the locomotive garage (where it was presumably parked). The buildings are classic examples of the decade's architecture and did not endure into the 21st century! An additional building was built to the left of the compressor in this view, with a substantial dry stone wall base. The site was also tidied up in later years of operation. Three very good photographs of the site, which were unavailable for this book, can be seen on the excellent Adit Now website and mining forum online.

Left: A later view of the mine entrance at Cornish Hush revealing not only the Greenbat locomotive and a short rake of Hudson 'U' skips, but also the considerable amount of work that had taken place to create the dry stone wall revetment and re-define the adit mouth and archway.

This map was discovered amongst papers held in the Beamish archive and reveals a geological map of the mines to the south of Bollihope and north of the Tees. The date and cartographer are not recorded, but it may have been used on the estate, as the boundaries of interests are shown prominently along with the veins and mines themselves. Note the Cornish Hush vein, running north west to south east, the Horse Level heading running into this (not shown) from the adit mouth at Cornish Hush itself. It is interesting that it does not show the earlier workings on the Hawkwood Burn.

This may date the map to the 1970s when SAMUK's operation was based at Cornish Hush. Some of the labelling appears to be applied by ball point pen, occasionally over pencil. With regard to the Cornish Hush vein itself, comparison with the Ordnance Survey map shows a series of mine shafts running along the vein as far as Black Hill, where a series of levels eventually cut across it. The route of the tramway followed the Howden Burn north eastwards towards Bollihope, but is not shown on this map (again as it was probably long since defunct when the map was created).

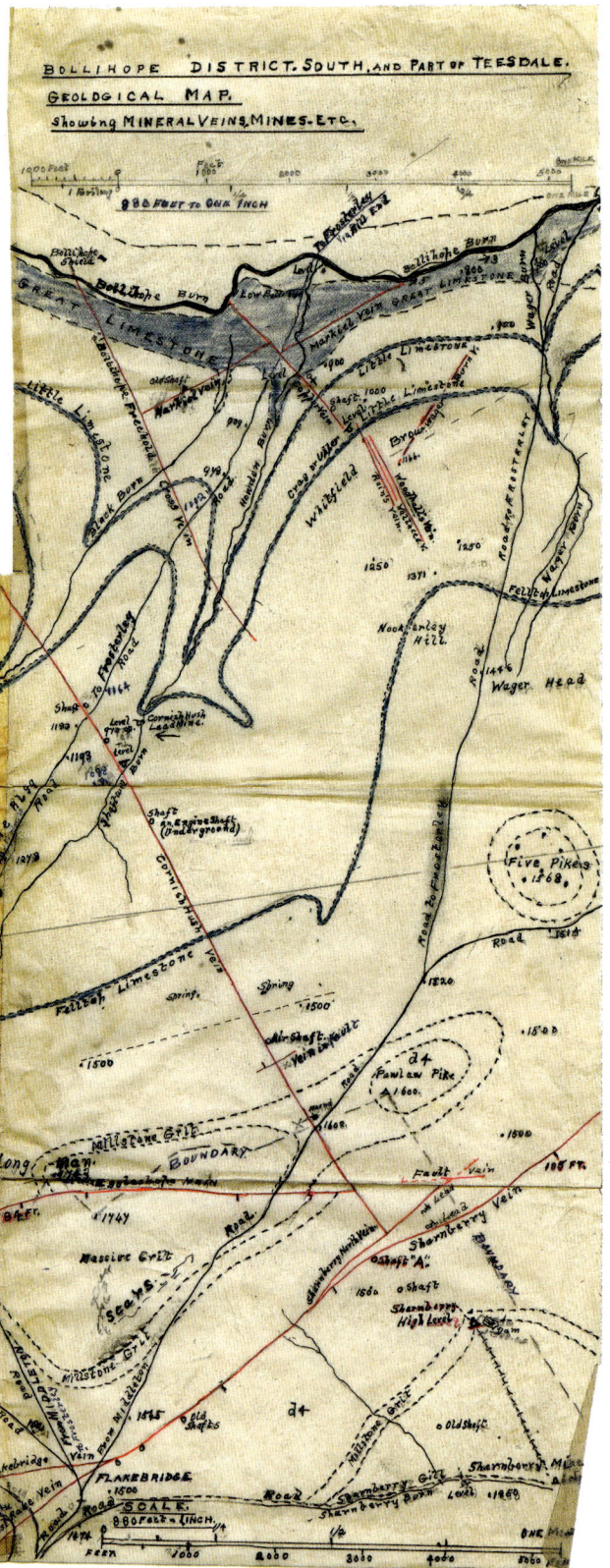

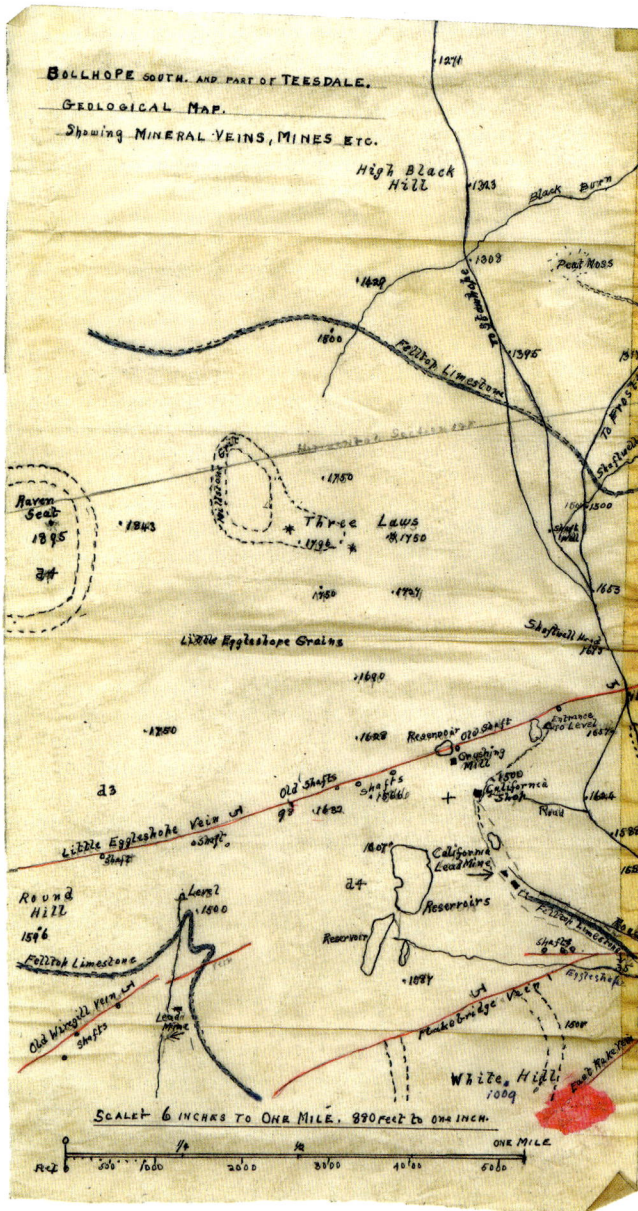

CHAPTER 2
THE ROUTE OF THE TRAMWAY

The first view is taken standing in the area of the Horse Level entrance to the mine at Cornish Hush looking in a north easterly direction across the large level area where the mine shop (workshop) was located (to the left of this view) and an array of sidings enabled waste to be sent to the tips whilst ore was sent down the tramway to Whitfield Brow. The large chasm running through this view is the first encounter the route makes with the Howden Burn, which has eroded a great deal of this area away and continues to do so at such a rate as to suggest it was perhaps originally culverted in this location in order to contain and control its flow. Map reference: NY998334

THE CORNISH HUSH TRAMWAY was a short and nearly level route of just over one mile in length from adit mouth (Cornish Hush Horse Level) to the crushing mill at Whitfield Brow. It did possess a number of interesting features in this brief run along the western flank of Nookerley Hill, the earthworks for all of which survive to enable examination today. Studying the route on the ground is relatively straightforward and the area is accessible to the walker (in 2016). What is more complex is trying to precisely date its construction, use and demise using Ordnance Survey Maps. This chapter, therefore, takes a sedate journey along the route, identifying the features of note along the way. Six digit Ordnance Survey references are used and distances have been shown in both miles and kilometres.

Shake Holes

Spring

Old Quarry

Bollihope Shield

Burn

B o l l i h o p e

900

Old Shaft

Bollihope

Ford

F.B.

Spring

800

Spring

Old Shaft

Lead Crushing Mill
(Disused)

1000

Moor Rigg
Spring

Air Shaft

Camperdown

Shake Holes

Old Quarry

B.M. 845·9

924

Old Level

Spring

Reservoir

Spring

Old Quarry

F.P.

Shake Hole

Spring

B.M. 913

900

TRAMWAY

Brow

B.M. 1156·4

Whitfield Brow Lead Mines

TRAMWAY

Whitfield

Quarry

B.M. 1156·4

1168

Old Quarries

Old Level

Old Quarry

978

1000

Old Level

Black

Burn

Howden Burn

1000

B.M. 1041·7

Old Level

1247

1250

Blackhill Spring

Old Level

Nookerley Hill

· Spr

· 1392

This map is reconstructed from 1898
Edition (six inch series) Ordnance
Survey sheets – Durham XXXII.NW
and Durham XXXII.SW.

F.P.

1155

1164

Old Shaft

Old Level

Level
Spring

Cornish Hush
Lead Mines

Quarry

Air Shaft

1193

Old Shafts

Cornish Hush

Hawkn

Old Quarries

Ruin

Currick

Spring

F.P.

F.P.

F.P.

1242

Fine Rigg

1266

Old Shafts

Green Sike

Reservoirs

Ford

Spring

Spring

1500

F.P.

Spring

1250

Old Quarry

Old Shaft

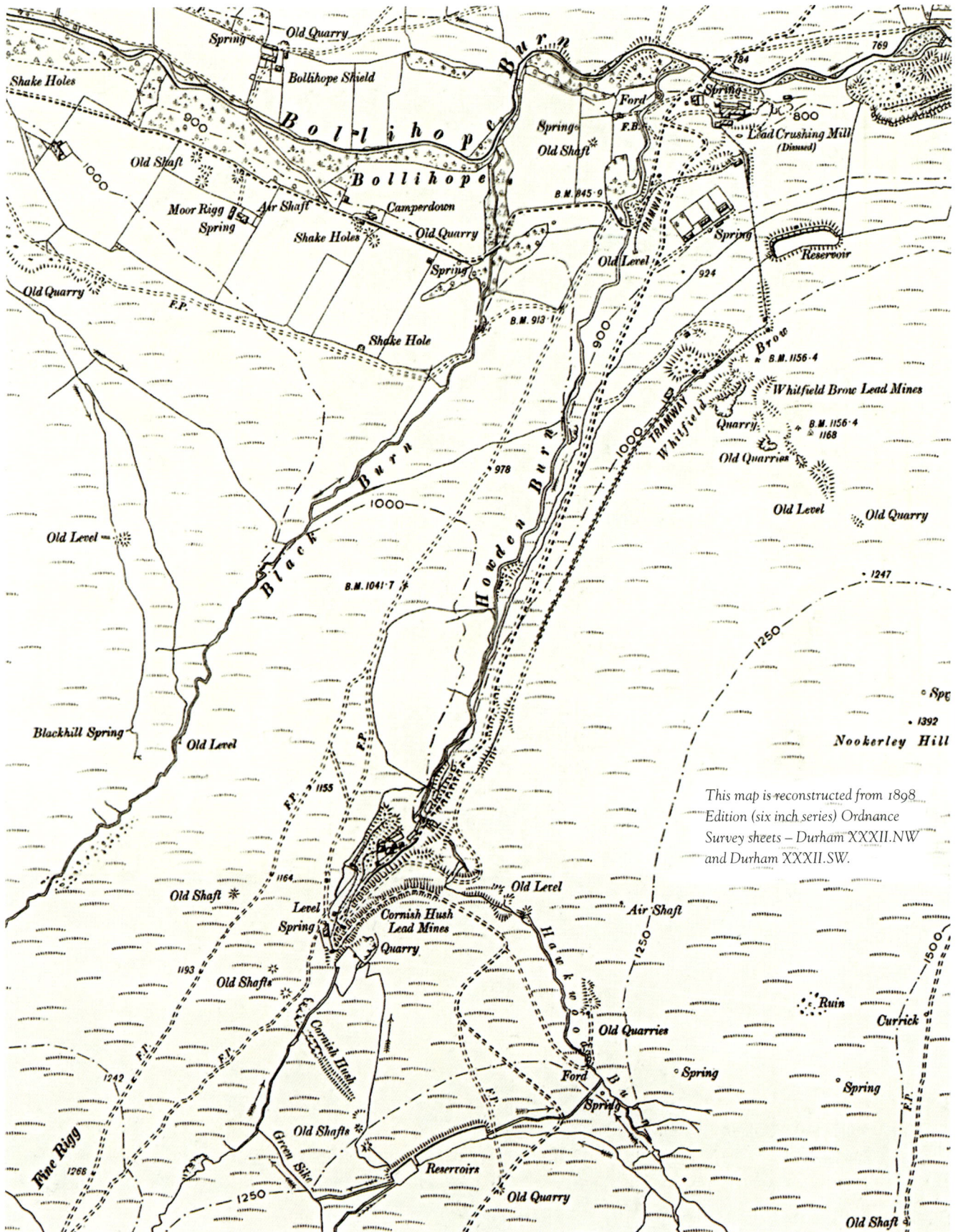

Above: Looking back to the level area in a south westerly direction, the site of the adit being at the extreme left of this view. The 1970s fluorspar activities undertaken by SAMUK were largely centred on this area, with numerous buildings being constructed to provide a locomotive garage, laboratories and stores for the (ultimately unsuccessful) prospecting work. Hudson Jubilee track was used, some lengths of which can be identified in the surrounding area, not least in fence construction. The rapidly collapsing canyon being carved by the Howden Burn in the foreground has, interestingly, revealed several T rail sections and some chairs, which date from the first period of activity at Cornish Hush.

Some explanation of 'hushing' may be of interest, as the Cornish Hush itself is located just to the south of the adit on the hillside above. Hushing was a process by which dams were constructed and large volumes of water stored in temporary reservoirs. These would then be released, their flow controlled to scour away a channel through over the vegetation and subsoil to expose the rock below. This was then scrutinised for veins of minerals into which headings and shafts could be driven. The process is one that was utilised as far back as the Romans, and evidence of it can be seen across the North Pennines to this day. Map reference: NY999335

The Horse Level entrance (NY998334) was just below the 330 metre contour line and the site of the incline summit is between the 310 and 320 metre contour. The incline then descends until the route becomes indistinct today but where the site of the mill was located at Whitfield Brow is around 250 metres above sea level.

The modern explorer can readily gain access to the route of the tramway, with parking available alongside the Bollihope Burn on the road from Frosterley across to the B6278. It should be noted that the area is used for game hunting and that paths should be adhered to and notices complied with. The adit mouth of Cornish Hush mine has long been obscured, though the position is evident at the point the private road makes a U turn as it climbs out of the valley. The Ordnance Survey Explorer map OL31 covers this area in detail and considerable information can be gleaned from the historical sequence of maps available via the Durham County Council website 'Keys to the Past' and searching under 'Bollihope' then 'maps'.

The journey along the tramway described here follows that of the loaded waggons of ore, starting at Cornish Hush as they break into daylight and begin the journey down the valley of the Howden Burn to the processing mill at Whitfield Brow.

Left upper: Looking west from the previous vantage point, large tips mark the landscape as an industrial one and demonstrate the colossal quantities of material which had to be extracted in order to remove relatively modest quantities of useful mineral ore. These tips actually date from the 1970s SAMUK operation, as they are still very clean and free of vegetation (and ore!) and are well aligned for the short sidings from Cornish Hush that are indicated on the 1970s editions of the Ordnance Survey for this area. The SAMUK operation did not utilise the route of the tramway, as the site was well-served by the route of the improved road (which runs south westwards from Bollihope to access a large acreage of the moors in this part of the Pennines) which is just visible in the bottom of this photograph.

Map reference: NY999335

Left lower: Remaining in the same spot but now turning to face the north east, the route of the tramway becomes very clear, running along the threshold of grassland and moorland heather on Nookerley Hill and following an almost level contour as it does so. Also notable is the road, a private track which was made passable for vehicles in more recent years (probably in association with the SAMUK operation at Cornish Hush but also used for management of the moorland and game) but would appear to have earlier origins as a route from south west to north east through this area. It probably also served as a pack-horse route for lead ore from the numerous mines across the moors, including Cornish Hush, arriving at a confluence of tracks at Bollihope where the crushing mills were located on the Bollihope Burn there.

Map reference: NY999335

Right: At a distance of 0.14 miles (0.23KM) from the adit mouth the tramway reaches its first notable feature. This is a junction where the route divides, apparently to serve a mine in the valley of the Hawkwood Burn, which flows from the south east to join the Howden Burn just to the north west of the tramway in this location. There are remaining spoil tips fanning away from the diverging route and a water course running within a carved stone channel. Map reference: NY000335

Below: The most significant and impressive feature on the route is this sizable embankment, built of waste and crossing the small valley through which the Hawkwood Burn passes before joining the Howden Burn just beyond the embankment in this view. The Hawkwood Burn runs through a stone lined culvert, as seen at its base, though in recent years this has been extensively eroded causing the embankment to collapse in ever increasing quantities. Beyond the embankment can be seen the tips illustrated earlier, and atop it can be seen the route of the tramway. Map reference: NY000335

Left: This is the embankment from the other side and shows both its scale but also the extensive damage to its structure caused in recent years by heavy rains and its inevitable obstruction (it is, in effect, a dam) of the Hawkwood Burn.

Map reference: NY000335

Below: A view of the embankment (not unlike Cei Mawr on the Ffestiniog Railway) looking north from a vantage point on the branching route seen earlier. One theory for this arrangement of routes is that the tramway originally curved eastwards following the contour (and therefore the diverging route was the sole route at one time), before touching upon the adit (serving a separate lead mine level) on the Hawkwood Burn, before regaining the contour and following the bluff of the hillside to regain what is the current route evident today. Perhaps as a result of the arrival of a steam locomotive, or the closure of that level, the embankment was constructed to provide a more direct and far less sinuous route across the valley mouth and to regain the route along Nookerley Hill towards Whitfield Brow?

Map reference: NY000335

Above: This view is taken from the surviving adit mouth on the Hawkwood Burn and shows the relatively compact nature of the features so far described. The burn runs below, whilst the embankment can be seen to the right. The theory regarding the contour route is very hard to quantify given the disruption to the land surface here and the absence of any crossing of the burn. However, the path to the right of this view does gradually reach the tramway route to the north east of the embankment and so could plausibly have carried the original tramway in its earliest phase. Of note are the smaller spoil tips, this view looking towards the south west.
Map reference: NY001334

Right: The surviving adit mouth which accessed a lead mine level on the Hawkwood Burn.
Map reference: NY001334

Three views of the tramway route as it settles down to follow the hillside from Cornish Hush to Whitfield Brow. The first view, looking south west, reveals a distinct path to the left of it, possibly the original route of the tramway based on the theory that it followed the contour into the Hawkwood Burn valley rather than crossing on the later embankment. It might also be a well-trodden route for game hunters or a pack horse route to the mine in the Hawkwood Burn valley. The other views show how the tramway marks the change in vegetation between grass and heather and how it is almost level throughout its route. An important point of note as SAMSON, based on the single photograph taken at Cornish Hush, faced north east. A locomotive would usually be arranged to face uphill, and usually the uphill route of a valley is towards the source rather than away, so clearly the gradient was not of any concern when the locomotive was placed on the rails in 1874.

Map reference: NY001337

Above: In a number of locations along the tramway route small embankments or revetments have been made to ensure its continuity. This is one of the most substantial and remains readily identifiable despite the passage of nearly 12 decades since it was used last.

Map reference: NY001337

Right: Looking south west the tramway can be seen as it begins its turn towards the incline summit above Whitfield Brow, 0.78 miles (1.26KM) from the mine entrance at Cornish Hush. In the area to the right of the tramway, as seen here, was a building (purpose unknown). There are large spoil tips to the right of this view, associated with the quarry operation on the hillside above, these being shown as the Whitfield Brow lead mines and quarries on the 1894 Ordnance Survey map.

Map reference: NY005343

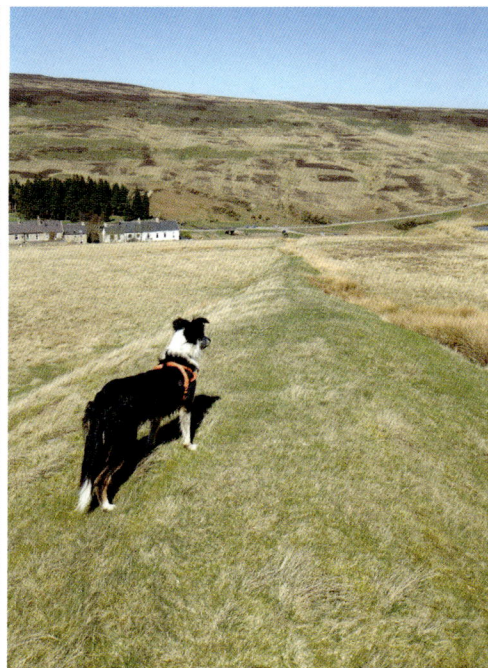

Above left: Travelling a hundred yards or so further along the tramway and looking south west, the full extent of the spoil tips can be seen, and likewise the trackbed of the tramway as it arrives into view. This photograph was taken standing at the top of the trackbed for the incline and so this area was the limit of horse and locomotive operations, 0.85 miles (1.42KM) from Cornish Hush.　　　　　　　　　　　　　　　　　　　　　*Map reference: NY006345*

Above right: Sam, the author's Border Collie (and not named after the locomotive!) stands on the incline trackbed looking across to Whitfield Brow and the remains of quite extensive quarry operations to the south of Bishopley. The road crossing of the Bollihope Burn is clearly visible, though the actual site of the lead mill is

obscured. The houses visible form the hamlet of Whitfield Brow, this area in general being known as Bollihope, after the Burn which was once forded (and is now bridged) here.
Map reference: NY006345

Right: This view, taken from the base of the incline and looking east north east shows the wide expanse at Bollihope, the site of the lead processing mill (foreground) and the quarries (middle distance, right). Today the site is a popular one with tourists, many parking to paddle or explore the quarries, some to venture further up the valleys that meet at this location. A large caravan park has been built here and so the lost sound of industry has been replaced by that of day-trippers and holidaymakers.
Map reference: NY006348

Mention was made earlier of the occasional revelation of tramway rails and chairs from the tramway era when flooding and washouts occur at the Cornish Hush end of the route. Here is one example, showing the T section wrought iron rail and an intermediate chair. These appear to be pegged with wooden dowels, presumably onto wooden sleepers, there being no evidence of stone sleepers anywhere in the area. Wider chairs have also been revealed, these acting to join rail lengths together, there being no fishplates fitted.

A sample of track components from the tramway era at Cornish Hush are kept at Beamish, including a single chair, doubled joining chair and a few short lengths of rail. As the latter have not survived intact, the actual rail length cannot be accurately determined, though other examples elsewhere would suggest a length of 15 ft. is likely. Rail weight is around 20lb per yard.

The single chairs perform their function in supporting the T section rail (rolled wrought iron with a flat bottom profile along its length), though unusually seemed to be secured to the rails using a peg, possibly metallic. This would appear to be in place of a conventional wooden key.

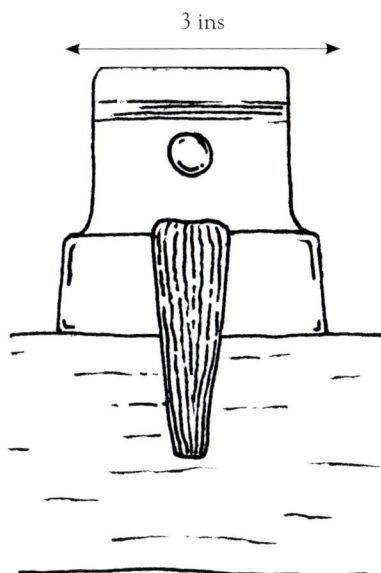

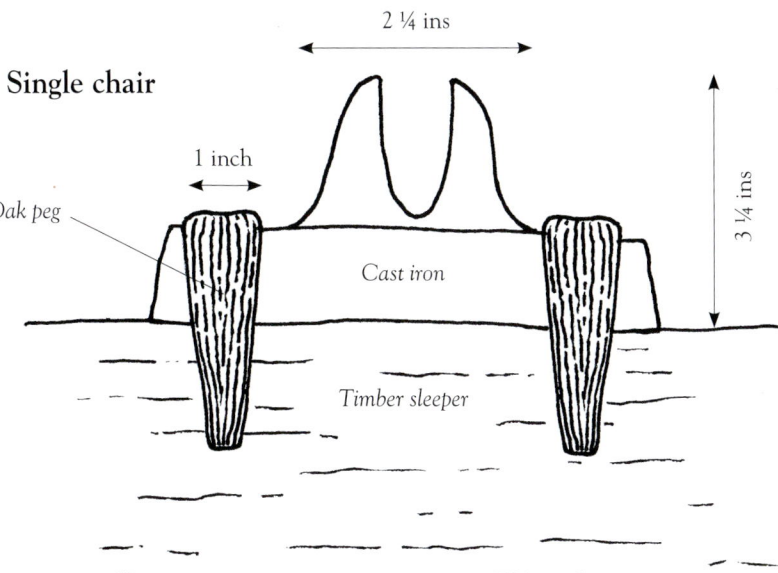

3 ins

Single chair

2 ¼ ins

3 ¼ ins

Oak peg

1 inch

Cast iron

Timber sleeper

Drawing by Paul Jarman©

Dimensions noted are for the track parts as they survive, it might be presumed that they were rounder numbers than they are now in their corroded condition.

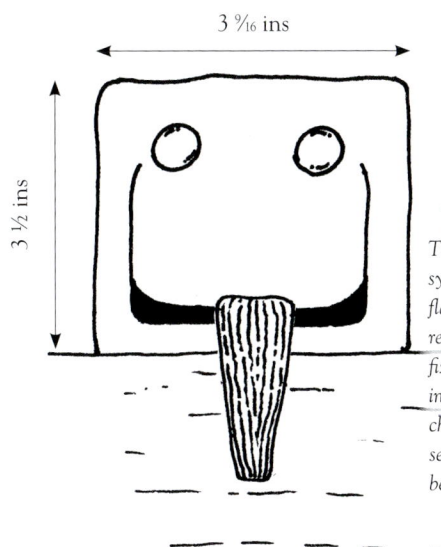

3 ⁹⁄₁₆ ins

3 ½ ins

Double 'joining' chair

The Joining chair is not symmetrical, one side being flatter than the other. A rebate allows for the peg fixing it to the sleeper to be inserted. As with the single chairs, the rails are held secure using what appears to be a metallic peg or rivet.

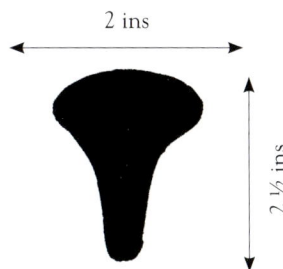

2 ins

2 ½ ins

Rail Section

RAIL SECTION & CHAIRS

To date, no evidence in any form has come to light regarding pointwork used at Cornish Hush. Overall the design of the track is very similar to that employed on the Welsh tramways at Gorseddau and Croesor (much of which was second hand from the Ffestiniog Railway).

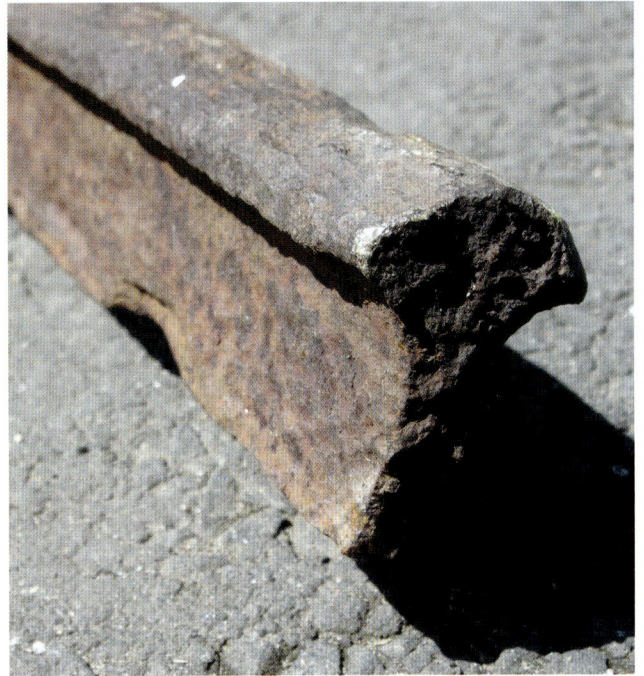

CHAPTER 3
STEPHEN LEWIN AND THE POOLE FOUNDRY – THE FIRST SAMSON

A close up view of SAMSON taken from the single original image and which gave the project to recreate the locomotive so much critical information. By creating a scale of known or 'best guess' dimensions, this view was able to give David Young the basic information needed to produce a new set of drawings of SAMSON. Differences will be noted, and are alluded to later on.

QUITE WHAT THE LINK between a foundry in the south of England and a remote County Durham lead mine was; or how, what even by the standards of the day, an unconventional steam locomotive came to be supplied to work on a mine tramway seated within hill country still wed to horse traction or manpower, may never be known.

It is a similar mystery to that which saw the same maker supply a steam locomotive to the Londonderry Railway (later Seaham Harbour Dock Company) for use at their coal-shipping harbour on the north east coast to the south of Sunderland in 1877. Perhaps the same connection existed to cause both sales and perhaps the sea trading routes, the equivalent of the modern motorways, enabled easier communications around the coastal waters of the United Kingdom than we perhaps today appreciate.

The Seaham locomotive, which became No.18, was to gain a degree of fame in the 1960s, entering its 89th year in the harbour's service before being withdrawn and later preserved at Beamish; but the earlier locomotive gained no such fame, almost certainly being

Above: As useful as the photograph, this engraving from 'The Engineer' in 1875 reveals the arrangement of the geared drive and also that both wheelsets were fitted with gear rings. Those fitted to the front axle are redundant and the possible reasons for this are discussed within the text. The new SAMSON's wheelcentre was reduced in the cast crankpin area in order to minimise the mass of metal needed (susceptible to deformation when cast) and also the length of the axle to be pressed into the casting. The engraving reveals some errors, the most noticeable being the step in the frame extensions where they fit around the bunker. The boiler cladding is also fitted differently to the manner of attachment revealed by the photograph – unless it was different on each side, which would be a very untidy arrangement.

consigned for scrap in 1904 and even then perhaps having been out of use for some time before that date. One can speculate, but it is perhaps better to deal in the facts and remain grateful that such trades took place for they enrich this history immeasurably.

In hindsight it is a little unjust that the name Stephen Lewin has become that so closely, and singly, associated with the small number of locomotives constructed at the Poole Foundry. It was in fact the work of the William James Tarrant, who took over as works manager after the separation of Stephen Lewin from his business partner William Wilkinson, that led to the creation of these distinctive little steam locomotives. But to understand the origins, we must first look back to 1863 when Stephen Samuel Lewin, an architect from Boston in Lincolnshire formed a business partnership with a local agricultural engineer named William Wilkinson.

In 1841, one William Pearce purchased land at Baiter Green in Poole, Dorset, with the intention of establishing a foundry and engineering works to produce agricultural implements. The business prospered and the foundry was expanded incrementally until 1863 when Pearce decided to sell the establishment. At this point Lewin and Wilkinson arrived on the scene, Lewin making the financial arrangements and remaining in Boston whilst Wilkinson moved to Poole to run the business.

A complex sequence of political events brought Lewin to Poole in 1866, ostensibly to take control of his brother's timber business. The foundry, trading as Lewin, Wilkinson & Co was about to undergo another change in management due to Wilkinson's involvement in a scandal involving the operation of a steamer service from Poole to Cherbourg and irregularities with the accounts at the foundry. Wilkinson was later declared bankrupt, his personal financial troubles also being reflected in the foundry's affairs, which were further complicated by a request from the financial backer to foreclose the mortgage by which Lewin had been able to purchase the works.

At the time of SAMSON's construction the workforce consisted of around two hundred men and boys (some of whom also worked in Lewin's timber yard), the company by now being named after its owner. In the spring of 1874 these men found themselves with a new boss, a young man named William Tarrant. He brought with him the experience of an apprenticeship with Brown & May, a portable and traction engine manufacturer from Devizes in Wiltshire. His legacy was to be crystallised in the steam locomotive output of the works over the next four years, his energy being rapidly focussed on the design and construction of the locomotive that would become SAMSON and was completed in the autumn of that same year.

LEWIN, POOLE, DORSET.

SPECIALITIES.

CONTRACTORS'
AND
COLLIERY
Locomotives

Locomotives for
use instead of
Horses on Narrow
Gauge and Light
Rails.

PORTABLE, FIXED,
AND VERTICAL
ENGINES,
The Cheapest and Simplest in the
Trade.

STREET AND ROAD
Tramway
Locomotives
ON THE MOST
IMPROVED
PRINCIPLES.

The above represents one of LEWIN'S STEEL GEARED LOCOMOTIVES, working on a 22-inch Gauge.   831

Above: Given the scarcity of photographs and images of SAMSON, the views that have survived have proved to be essential in the recreation of the new locomotive. Taken from 'Engineering' for the 6 October 1876, this advert reveals some confidence in the design in that it is still being promoted over a year since the original SAMSON was delivered despite no further apparent orders for the type being forthcoming (this would change in 1877 when the similar HOPS and MALT were supplied to Guinness). This engraving creates some confusion with regard to the design of the boiler and appearance of the backhead however. The way in which this is depicted suggests a locomotive type boiler is fitted, due to the depth of the rear plate and way in which it descends all the way to the footplate floor. There are also two plugs which appear to be washout plugs low down and to each side of this plate. Imagining a few invisible lines onto the engraving does create a problem with its rendition as the firebox could not be as wide as depicted, unless it formed part of the rear section of the frames – something the Ffestiniog Railway George England built locomotives featured a decade earlier. There is also a problem in finding any space for an ashpan, damper or even any clearance underneath the locomotive for the bottom of the firebox and its foundation ring. Comparison with the photograph further undermines this notion as the result would be a firebox so short as to be of little use in creating steam. It might therefore be reasonably assumed that there is some artistic licence at play here, and that the backhead is not an accurate depiction of what really existed. But maybe another photograph will come to light and prove the new SAMSON is wrong after all…

Tarrant left the company in 1878, coinciding with the end of locomotive building at the Poole Foundry. This was not the company's first blow in that decade however, for on the 30th April 1876 a fire broke out and devastated a large portion of the works, destroying partly-built yachts and stockpiles of agricultural machinery (one of the main areas of production at the works). As a result of the fire it seems agricultural work was phased out and work on locomotives became the main focus of manufacture. Tarrant's departure and an economic downturn conspired to further undermine the fortunes of the business, and in 1884 Stephen Lewin was declared bankrupt, the remaining contents of the works being auctioned in September of that year.

Stephen Lewin drifted into the history books but his name was not to be forgotten and would live on largely due to the extended life of No.18 at Seaham Harbour and the book on the man, foundry and their products written by Russell Wear and Eric Lees in 1978.

THE FIRST SAMSON
The earliest documentary record of SAMSON is in the *Poole Herald*, dated 17 December 1874 and reporting 'Mr Lewin has just sent

away to be worked in a lead mine a small locomotive…' Further media coverage was to be found in *The Engineer, Engineering* and the *Mining Journal*. The latter's report, dating from January 1875, is worth mentioning in full:

The above illustration [see the engraving] represents a small geared tramway engine for the working of narrow gauge tramways, in the place of horse labour, designed by Mr. S. Lewin, of the Poole Iron Works, Dorset. The design is very simple, and it certainly possesses very many advantages over the double cylinder direct-acting loco for small powers. It is not so complicated, and the whole of the working parts are kept well up out of the way of dirt or any obstructions, while the gearing is very strong and of cast steel, rendering it very durable and not liable to injury. The engine can be easily handled, and no difficulty is experienced from the engine getting on its centres. One of these engines was supplied last autumn to the London Lead Mining Co. of Middleton in Teesdale, and they report that "as a substitute for horse labour the engine is answering its object most satisfactorily," and they also say "we consider the design and workmanship very good and can confidently recommend them for tramway work." The engine which they here refer to is of the 2½ n.h.p. type and weighs in working order 2 tons 12cwt.

The paragraph above is very interesting. The reference to the 'engine getting on its centres' refers to the tendency of a single cylinder engine to require careful positioning of the piston (in order to place the engine on its 'starting stroke'). The claim therefore that no difficulty is presented must therefore refer to the experience of the operator rather than some particular feature of the design itself. The reference to n.h.p. refers to nominal horse power, again a term familiar from traction engine and agricultural engineering practice and at odds with the now accepted railway norm for Tractive Effort (TE) or Indicated Drawbar Horse Power (IDHP).

It is possible that the Poole Foundry of Stephen Lewin did build a locomotive before SAMSON, works number 551. This was listed in the general number series (as all of the locomotives were so allocated) and was described as a single cylinder 6¼ inch 4 hp portable engine. John Fletcher researched this locomotive (believed to be a 0-4-0WT arrangement) and published his findings in issue seven of Archive magazine, proposing a construction date of 1873 for this locomotive. Tantalisingly, two later locomotives supplied from Poole were also described as '4 hp portable engines'. No.551 was supplied to work on the White Brothers cement works tramway at Swanscombe, Kent, running on 3 ft 6 in gauge tracks and featuring outside flanges on its wheels. Its life was short and so by 1880 it was declared 'useless', though some parts may have been incorporated into a locomotive assembled at the works at a later date.

Lewin's own sales literature described their 'Tramway Locomotive Engines' in the following terms:

> 'I make these of two kinds, one suitable for drawing weights up to about 35 tons at a speed of about five miles per hour on very narrow gauge lines to replace horse power. The other kind I make is a simple form of direct-acting Contractor's Locomotive to draw weights from 40 to 150 tons on gauges varying from 2 ft 6 ins to 5 ft 1 ins.'

The latter direct acting locomotive was the format to which the Seaham Harbour engine (No.18) was built when supplied to the Londonderry Railway in 1877. There is only one known photograph of SAMSON, showing the engine at Cornish Hush. See page viii and 20 (enlarged detail). As photographs go, it is extremely useful, revealing an almost dead-on side view. There are also two engravings, showing the rear three quarter view of the locomotive and an opposite side view to that in the photograph.

It is an opportune moment to consider the engravings, or rather their creation, themselves, along with the teasing realisation that they were almost certainly created by copying photographs. Magazines and advertisers would commission engravers to produce artwork for publications, and this could be a largely desk-bound

practice once photography had been established. The practice continued as photographs could not be reproduced directly, but they could be used as a base image to copy. Therefore, did photographs of SAMSON exist showing the gear (left hand) side and rear three quarter view, and if so, what became of them? Indeed, an 1877 advert shows the latter engraving and noting it to be 'from a photograph of a steel geared engine'. There are photographs of new locomotives taken in the works yard, so perhaps these were supplied as prints to engravers – in which case there are (or were) images somewhere of SAMSON in Poole before it was delivered to Cornish Hush.

WHAT THE IMAGES REVEAL

The boiler (of approximately 2 ft diameter and 8 ft in length) was most likely of a non-depending marine design, with a small furnace tube fitted inside the main barrel, with the fire tubes running forwards from this to the tubeplate and with the rear end supported by the backhead. A very simple design, with no stays and of the type used on the Crewe 18 in locomotives and later, the Horwich Works narrow gauge locomotives built by and for the LNWR and L&Y respectively. This design was additionally used with aplomb by Sir Arthur Heywood in his 15 in gauge locomotives. This is also the type of boiler fitted to the three Beamish replica locomotives: STEAM ELEPHANT, PUFFING BILLY and LOCOMOTION NO.1.

Critical accessories to the boiler, in the case of SAMSON, are the crankshaft, motion and cylinder block. These were carried atop the boiler on cast iron pedestals, and though the best evidence is again the engravings, the photograph does give quite a clear indication of the arrangement as well.

A pair of slide bars/guides carried the piston rod/little-end and appear to have been supported on a boiler mounted bracket at their outer end. Stephenson Link motion was fitted, and the reversing lever can be seen in the forward position in the photograph, with the forward eccentric rod to the fore and lifting links lowered accordingly. The engravings suggest that a marine type big end bearing was employed on Samson. Lewins were of course established marine engine manufacturers.

Situated above and slightly behind the rear axle is the crankshaft, with the flywheel prominent in the photograph. The engravings confirm a typical arrangement, from right to left, of flywheel, bearing pedestal, pump eccentric, valve eccentric, big end, bearing block and pinion. Whether or not this pinion could be disengaged or not is the source of some discussion – ideally it would disengage to enable the pump to operate whilst the locomotive was stationary as well as enable the locomotive to belt-drive machine tools as required (two later Lewin-built narrow gauge locomotives – HOPS and MALT – supplied to the Guinness Brewery in Dublin were latterly used almost entirely as rail mounted portable engines – see photograph on page 24).

Below: Without a doubt the closest locomotives in design to Samson were HOPS and MALT, whose image was captured in the yard at Poole and usefully showed the engines facing each other and thus revealing both sides of this variant on Lewin's overtype design. Built in 1877 and fitted with 6¼ in x 8 in cylinders, the pair weighed in at five tons apiece – sufficient to give them the required adhesion needed for the tramway around Guinness Brewery's St James' Gate site in Dublin and which featured a spiral tunnel with a gradient of 1 in 39 on a continuous radius of 61 ft 4 in.

Right: Though HOPS and MALT were of a useful weight, it was unsprung and the pair were said to have damaged the track, as a result both engines were relegated to portable engine status, where their flywheels would be connected via belts to static machinery and plant. HOPS was scrapped in 1914 whilst MALT endured for another 13 years beyond this. This very grainy image originates from the 'The Locomotive Magazine', April 1902.

Photo: Collection Andrew Neale

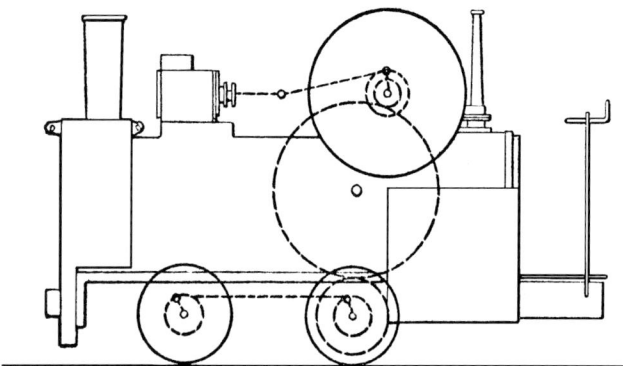

"*Geared engines, as shown above, were then procured, weighing about 5 tons, and owing to their increased hauling power were found very useful; but the absence of springs rendered them costly in repairs and hard on the road. They were slow in speed and somewhat troublesome in starting.*"

From Engineering Magazine, September 1888

In the photograph the water pump can just be discerned. This was driven from the crankshaft, the linkage being shown in the three-quarter rear view engraving. The photograph shows a lever at the rear of the pump, and study of the pipework would suggest this is the by-pass mechanism, enabling water not required for filling the boiler to be recirculated to the tank.

The frames appear to be full depth, swept at the front and slightly swept in depth to the rear of the rear axle. They did not continue to the rear of the locomotive, but the gap was bridged using slender frame extensions which were positioned at the extreme width of the locomotive, enveloping the bunkers and in line with the rear buffer beam. It is also possible that the engine was weighted at the front end, possibly marked by a feint line on the photograph to the bottom of the frame plate ahead of the leading driving wheels.

It is not readily apparent how the water tank(s) were accommodated within the frames. The new SAMSON has two tanks of equal size

LINDHOLME was the last of Lewin's overtype locomotives, built (probably) to standard gauge and notable for the widely spaced frames and internal gearing. The sole surviving photograph is unfortunately not of very high quality, but it is included here for its interest. With rumours of the engine surviving, buried in a clay pit, perhaps it might yet reveal the answers to the questions about the Poole Foundry's overtype design...

Photo: Collection Andrew Neale

and connected by a balance pipe. The tank structure also provides additional stiffening of the frame plates in this area.

It is presumed that SAMSON was not sprung. However, the axle bearings (axle boxes) may have been allowed a small degree of movement in their hornguides, possible cushioned on rubber 'springs' – a practice evident on the 1860s Crewe locomotives which Lewins must have been aware of, as well as contemporary rolling stock and something which was also incorporated into Beamish's replica of STEAM ELEPHANT.

SAMSON had four driving wheels of equal size and connected by coupling rods which featured circular bearings over the crankpins with a substantial circular section rod between of fishbelly profile. The wheels were cast steel, with integral (and profiled) cranks. The right hand side was of conventional style whilst the left hand side wheels incorporated a toothed gear, largely of hollow section (and therefore integral with the wheel centre casting?). The rear axle was driven (via an intermediate gear, though this is enclosed by a metal casing in the engravings), but the front axle also featured an integral gear on the left hand side.

This has been suggested as a possible economy to enable easy exchange of front and rear axles due to gear wear. However, this would not counter wear on the crankshaft pinion or intermediate gear and it would seem more likely that, if the gears are assumed to be cast integrally with the wheels, it was the cheapest expedient to create a stepped crankpin on the front axle. This was required in order to equally space the coupling rod for both of the coupled wheels, saving a pattern being made and also, if required, affording a means of swapping the gears around.

The footplate was a distinctive feature on SAMSON, being incredibly low and clearly of such construction as to preclude frame plates running the whole length of the loco. The brake rod is startlingly low and would appear from the photograph to foul the ground, and must have had only marginal clearance of turnouts etc. Given SAMSON's traction engine design, the reverser would be used

as an effective means of retarding the locomotive and so it could be assumed that the brake fitted was for parking purposes only. Many contemporary traction engines were not fitted with brakes at all and drivers habitually use the reversing lever for braking on nearly all road steam engines of conventional type.

Stephen Lewin built five overtype (Traction Engine Type) locomotives, beginning with SAMSON. It was two years before another followed, this being CROCODILE in 1876, supplied to the Northampton Gaslight Company where it ran for less than a decade before requiring overhaul whereupon it was relegated to spare engine duty until 1907.

In 1877 HOPS and MALT were supplied for use on the 1 ft 10 in narrow gauge system at the Guinness Brewery in Dublin, their specification, recounted by Wear and Lees, recording that they were fitted with a wrought iron clutch to enable the engine to be operated separately without the locomotive moving. Steam pressure was 140psi in a boiler constructed from Low Moor and Best Best [sic] (triple wrought) Staffordshire Iron. Interestingly it is also recorded that a chimney extension was utilised for steam raising and stationary work and that the water tanks (plural) were located between the frames. Each was supplied at a cost of £366, the footplate being additionally removable to aid their movement between levels around the brewery.

The final overtype built by Stephen Lewin as LINDHOLME, supplied to an estate on Hatfield Moors in East Yorkshire. Little else is known about this locomotive though rumours abound that its remains still exist at the bottom of a flooded clay pit, a story deriving some credibility from reports that it was observed along with several waggon wheelsets – borne out by an advert dating from 1883 offering a Lewin locomotive and 160 pairs of contractors waggon wheels for sale at this location. Maybe LINDHOLME does still exist and one day will be recovered and answer many of the questions raised about Lewin's locomotives and distinctive overtype design?

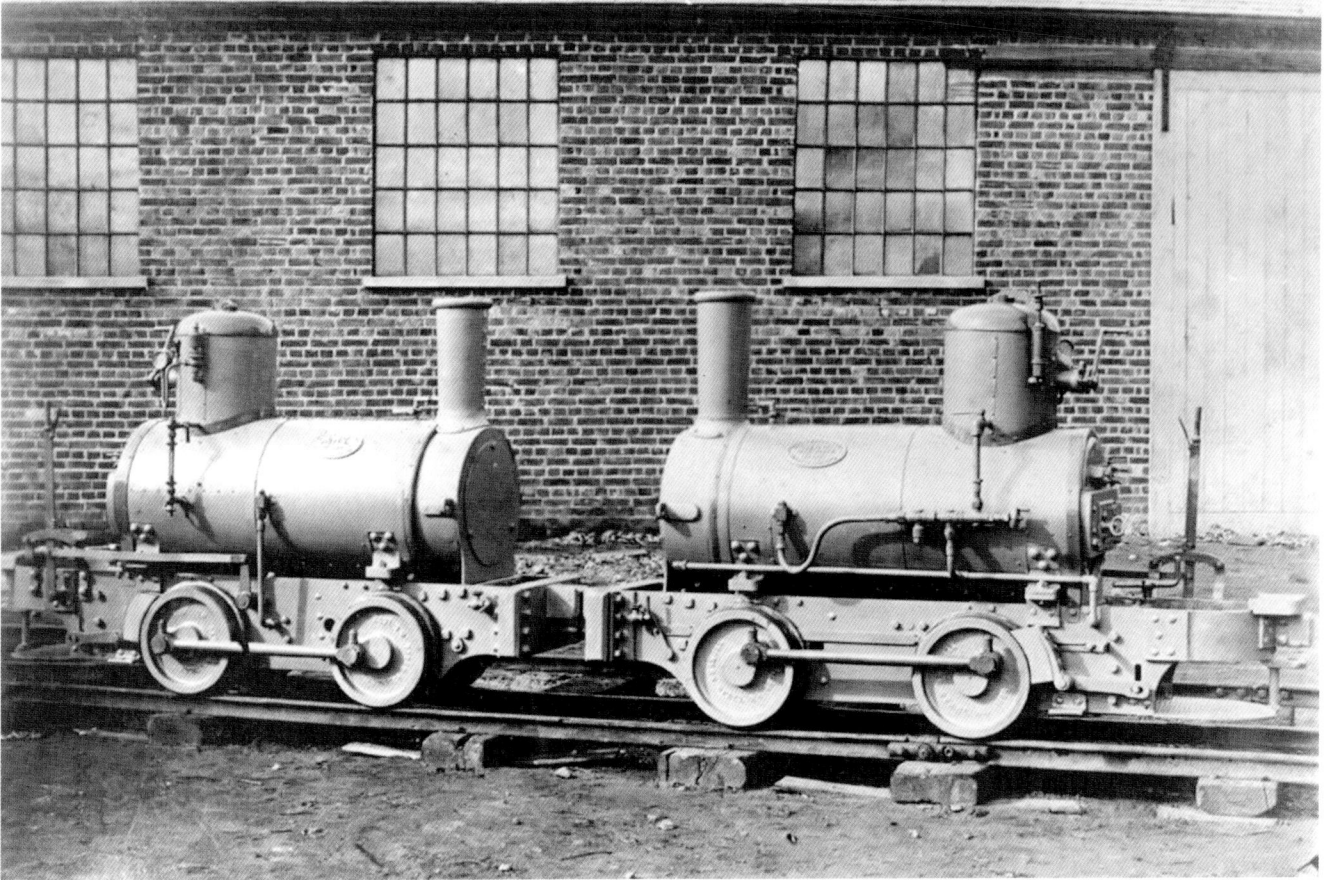

Above: Whilst not of overtype design, Lewin's 1877 0-4-0 locomotives ANT and BEE, supplied to the Great Laxey Mining Company Ltd on the Isle of Man, have many similar features to SAMSON. Fitted with non-depending boilers, they had two small cylinders between the frames which drove the rear axle and coupled wheels – set to a gauge of 1 ft 7 in They were extensively modified over their working lives, even being photographed with William Tarrant (the man who oversaw their construction) in 1921 before being sold for scrap in the mid-1930s. Both have subsequently been replicated, a pair being built in 2004 for the revived Great Laxey Mine Railway.

Right: In service, with the front water tank (not shown in the works photo) and side panniers for the carriage of coal, in place.

Photos: Collection Andrew Neale

Right: As an illustration of some of the other overtype traction engine locomotives produced, here is an example from Aveling & Porter at Rochester, Kent. Progress (6040 built in 1906) worked at Swanscombe Cement Works on the unusually gauged 3 ft 5½ in railway there. This was also the location where Lewin's first locomotive is thought to have worked. Note in particular the outside flanged wheels and not unfamiliar side profile of the locomotive. Note the twin-cylinder block, this engine being a compound (the 'simpling' valve to enable the low pressure cylinder to work at high pressure if the engine is on dead-centre being the upper of the rods running back to the footplate).

Photo: Collection Andrew Neale

Above left: Another Aveling machine, BLUE CIRCLE, was built in 1929 (works number 9449) and used at Snodland Cement Works until it was presented to the Bluebell Railway in 1964. Now owned by Michael Smith, it has been restored to its original blue livery and in 2010 appeared at Beamish on a working visit where it is seen on the industrial railway adjacent to The Pit Village. BLUE CIRCLE is very close in form to a traction engine, having larger driving wheels at the rear and smaller pony wheels beneath the smokebox. This gives it the wheel arrangement 2-2-0WT (well tanks being fitted beneath the boiler and bunker).

Above right: By way of contrast with BLUE CIRCLE, SIR VINCENT (8800/1917), also seen at Beamish in 2010, is of a more substantial and sophisticated design. It has four driving wheels, connected by gears (the rods between axle centres are not coupling rods), has two cylinders (being a compound, using the steam twice in one block with two connected bores) and it also has the luxury of a cab. Aveling & Porter built a respectable number of their traction engine locomotive designs for industrial users, and another example preserved is the 1872 built Wotton Tramway locomotive, No.1, the latter having a very similar silhouette to SAMSON another source of inspirations for Lewin's design?

Right: This wonderful standard gauge Fowler traction engine locomotive is thought to date from 1871 and features a single-cylinder engine and a very similar layout to SAMSON, albeit with the flywheel and gears reversed. The locomotive is also a three shaft machine like SAMSON – could this design have inspired Tarrant when he was laying out the Lewin locomotive in 1874?

Photo: Collection Andrew Neale

CHAPTER 4
SAMSON IN VICTORIAN NARROW GAUGE LOCOMOTIVE DESIGN CONTEXT

ONCE IT HAD BEEN DECIDED to build a new SAMSON for the 21st Century, the research into the original locomotive began, using the well-known sources described in Chapter 3, but also considering its peers, the contemporary sources available to the engineers at the Poole Foundry and the influences other narrow gauge locomotive designs might have imparted.

Before proceeding, it is perhaps useful to draw attention to some basic elements of SAMSON's design that will become relevant in the paragraphs that follow. SAMSON was a four-coupled locomotive, there being four wheels coupled together to impart motion from the cylinder (in this case via the crankshaft and second-shaft gears). It features a non-depending boiler (as described in the previous chapter) and was built to very compact proportions, perhaps with direct replacement of horse/pony traction in mind. It should also be remembered that the original SAMSON was 1 ft 10 in gauge – this sub-2 ft gauge being an important consideration in the comparisons drawn with a number of 15 in and 18 in gauge locomotives in this chapter.

SAMSON was by no means the first narrow gauge steam locomotive, nor can those which are described here claim this title. But it does belong to quite a small group of narrow gauge steam locomotives built to work as part of a process, be it mineral extraction or manufacturing, in the early to mid-Victorian period.

P. J. G. Ransom, in his book *Narrow Gauge Steam* described in detail the evolution of narrow gauge steam locomotives, and in particular what he called 'small' locomotives and this work is recommended to those wishing to study this subject in more detail. For the purposes of this narrative therefore, the earliest locomotive that might be considered influential in the design features utilised on SAMSON were the circa 30 0-4-0 single cylinder locomotives built by Neilson & Co in Glasgow to a variety of gauges and commencing in 1856.

They found favour in ironworks and heavy industry and featured a non-depending firebox in the boiler which ran almost the full length of the locomotive, with water carried in a tank placed on top of the boiler barrel. One of these locomotives would make for a very interesting new-build project, especially given their single-cylinder arrangement.

Another notable locomotive in this exploration, not least as it

was arranged to drive via gears, was created in 1861 when Isaac Watt Boulton rebuilt a standard gauge locomotive to 2 ft gauge before setting it to work on a mile-long tramway near Wigan. Named LITTLE GRIMSBY, it was rebuilt again in 1864 and re-gauged to 2 ft 8 in and was sold to the Weardale Iron and Coal Company where it worked at Tow Law Iron Works until retired and scrapped, possibly in the late 1880s.

The London & North Western Railway works at Crewe in Cheshire is a name synonymous with the 'big railway' and the industry of producing and maintaining a wide array of steam locomotives from 1843 to the present (there still being an important steam engineering facility in the town today). It is probably less well known for, what was at the time (1861), a revolutionary installation – an 18 in narrow gauge works railway, connecting workshops and stores around the complex and, for the first time, enabling efficient mobilisation of components as part of a 'process'.

The first locomotive on this system was designed by the LNWR's Chief Mechanical Engineer John Ramsbottom, who was something of a visionary for streamlined production at the time. Named, appropriately enough, TINY, there was nothing ironic about its name. It was scaled within the stature of a small pony, no wider than 3 ft wide, around 8 ft long and just over 7 ft to the top of the chimney (in modified form). There were four coupled wheels, the cylinders were located inside the frames and the water tank sat atop the boiler with clearance for the chimney and very capacious dome. The boiler itself was 2 ft diameter and just over twice as long. The firebox was very nearly half the length of the boiler, smokebox included, and was cylindrical in shape, supported by the horizontal tubes, themselves located into a conventional tubeplate at the front end.

The grate was formed of firebars running from the firehole doorplate forwards to a 'bridge', upon which a firebrick deflector was

Left and right: The Genesis of the 'compact' narrow gauge steam locomotive – PET, built in 1865, to the same design as TINY, remained 'stored' in the famous works Paint Shop at Crewe. This prolonged storage ensured that it survived into an era where it could be appreciated and it was moved to the Narrow Gauge Railway Museum at Tywyn. It now resides in the National Railway Museum at York, where this view was taken. The Crewe works tramways were closed in 1932, after a brief flirtation with diesel traction.

Below left: A close up view taken below the firebox of PET and which clearly demonstrates the advantage of a non-depending firebox design, enabling such a narrow gauge to accommodate a boiler wider than the track spacing. Also of note is the simple springing arrangement and very small driving wheels used on the Crew locomotives – 15¼ in diameter.

Below right: A view taken inside PET's firebox. The circular shape is obvious here. The brick bridge is substantial and without the firebars in position, dominates the view. The top row of tubes is just visible above this, there being 37 in total (coincidentally the same as the new Samson).

located. This had the effect of creating a small combustion area at the front of the firebox, free of debris from the fire and accessible via a removable plate located beneath the bridge. The simplicity of this design and ease with which it could be constructed would appear to have had a profound influence on Stephen Lewin's smaller designs. This is a point of view underpinned by the designs later built at Poole for, most notably, ANT and BEE supplied to work the Laxey Mines tramway, and HOPS and MALT for the Guinness Brewery

railway (all four built in 1877). Ramsbottom's Crewe design would also form the basis for a number of locomotives built by Sharp, Stewart, including an example supplied for use on the Guinness Brewery tramway, and the locomotives designed by Sir Arthur Heywood and Beyer Peacock that are examined now.

Once the non-depending boiler type (sometimes referred to as 'marine') had been settled on for the new SAMSON, then the similarity in dimensions to the locomotives designed and built by Sir

Below left: John Ramsbottom almost certainly influenced the design of two locomotives built by Sharp, Stewart at their Atlas Works, Manchester, in 1870 and then again in 1875. No.2079 was supplied for the 1ft 6½ ins gauge railway at the Ebbw Vale Steel, Iron & Coal Company Ltd in South Wales where it was named LITTLE DORRIT. It bore such a close resemblance to Ramsbottom's Crewe design that its origins cannot be in doubt. Ramsbottom had been an employee at the Atlas Works in 1839 so perhaps retained a friendly relationship with the firm and when approached for 18 in locomotives (which the LNWR would not have been willing to build) recommended his former employer? In 1875 the design was yet again dusted off, this time to produce a slightly modified 1 ft 10 in 0-4-0ST for the Guinness Brewery tramway, where it was given the first number in the series there. No.1 (works No. 2477) was not a great success as it was considered too light for the work around the extensive site and was later relegated to conveying passengers around the brewery in a pair of bench seat coaches. It was withdrawn in 1913. Dimensionally these locomotives follow the key measurements of the Crewe locomotives to such an extent that Sharp, Stewart must have had access to the LNWR drawings, perhaps via Ramsbottom himself?

Photos: Collection Andrew Neale

Arthur Heywood for his 15 in gauge Duffield Bank Railway became apparent. Heywood was a proponent of 15 in gauge as the narrowest practical gauge for a commercial or estate railway, above the point at which a railway might be considered a 'miniature' or 'toy' operation.

Sir Arthur Heywood began his minimum gauge experiments in 1874 (the year that SAMSON was built in Poole), its existence to a wider audience breaking cover in August 1877. Heywood would thereafter ensure that his minimum gauge experiments would not be attended by obscurity, though in turn he was influenced in his quest by the work of Charles Easton Spooner, a name inextricably associated with the Ffestiniog Railway, which had successfully modernised and adopted narrow gauge steam traction (alongside gravity) in 1863.

Heywood's first locomotive was EFFIE, completed in 1875 and of a conventional design in that it had four coupled wheels, outside cylinders, a domed boiler and rather resembled the outline of a diminutive steam locomotive such as a child might sketch. Heywood was acutely aware of maximising the adhesion of his Lilliputian locomotive, whence there were no trailing wheels, the balance of the locomotive through its combination of wheelbase and overhangs was exactly symmetrical and it was also fitted with a non-depending firebox so as not to impede the frame design to accommodate a conventional locomotive-type boiler.

Mark Smithers has written at length on the design developments made by Heywood and also the influences upon him by others, not

least the Royal Engineers, who in the 1870s were seeking a successful design of locomotive for their 18 in gauge military railways. Thus Heywood evolved his locomotive design into a larger side tank locomotive named ELLA, arranged on six coupled wheels. This set a form that gave a family resemblance to his remaining locomotives, and it was one of these, KATIE, which Beamish was able to study (and through the kindness of James Waterfield, obtain drawings for) which enabled Graham Morris to design a new boiler for SAMSON based on a known design and its principles.

The timeline of developments occupied by the earlier Crewe locomotives suggests that Stephen Lewin (or perhaps it was William Tarrant, as the works foreman and guiding hand for the Lewin locomotive style) had at least an awareness of these other locomotives and their builders. The similarly influenced Heywood family of engines, and the Horwich works 18 in gauge locomotives (built from 1887 by Beyer Peacock) is also readily apparent, and so they were also investigated during the design stages of the new SAMSON.

The firebox doorplate arrangement was, in particular, derived from the Horwich style, accepted as an evolution of both the Crewe and Heywood designs and therefore likely to be successful on the new SAMSON, whose boiler was so closely derived from the Heywood form. It cannot be known for certain if Lewin/Tarrant were aware of the Heywood locomotives and whether these influenced the designs which came after SAMSON, but they almost certainly encountered

Right: Sir Arthur Heywood's No.2 seen at Duffield Bank, revealing the details of its backhead with a great deal of clarity. Note the pair of gauge glasses (rather than one glass and a set of try-cocks as are often found in this period), both sans protectors. Also note the apparent absence of a damper plate. Taken in 1881, this stunning image first appeared in Heywood's Minimum Gauge Railways, a publication which explored and promoted the 15 in gauge railway as a practical proposition and described 'their application, construction and working' in various editions.

Left: URSULA was Heywood's final locomotive, seen here at work on the Eaton Hall Railway (on the estate of the Duke of Westminster) in 1931. It arrived at Eaton in 1895 and was scrapped in 1942. Part of the railway has been rebuilt at Eaton, complete with a replica of Katie and other Heywood rolling stock.

This photograph was also taken at Eaton Hall, showing 0-4-0T KATIE navigating the perimeter of the cricket ground with a trainload of coal for the estate's private power station. KATIE escaped scrapping and led something of a nomadic existence before its remains found their way to the Ravenglass & Eskdale Railway. A lengthy and detailed restoration began, which is now being completed by Station Road Steam in Lincolnshire.

Photos: Collection Jmes Waterfield

Above: James Waterfield has become a connoisseur of the minimum gauge as promoted by Sir Arthur Heywood, amassing a collection of original and replica rolling stock including a replica of 0-6-0T URSULA, seen here with an original Eaton Railway saloon car and matching replica bogie brakevan. This view readily demonstrates the similarity in size to SAMSON, so the serendipitous availability for SAMSON of a tried and tested boiler design, in a roundabout way, comes courtesy of Sir Arthur Heywood. The detail shows the backhead of the locomotive, complete with the neat cast iron firehole door surround.

Below left: This is KATIE's boiler, currently under restoration at Station Road Steam and where it was kindly made available for Graham Morris and the author to study during the design phase of SAMSON. The simple construction, with a riveted angle ring at the rear to which the backhead is fitted is apparent. Note the ring of rivets at the front which reveals the position of the front tubeplate. The dome is a feature not replicated on SAMSON (as the cylinder block fulfils this role in part) otherwise the boiler's design and dimensions are a very close to those of SAMSON.

Below right: This view shows KATIE's backhead and firebox. In this instance the firebox is welded to the backhead, but this apart, the design is more or less that perpetuated on the new SAMSON.

Photos: Collection Jmes Waterfield

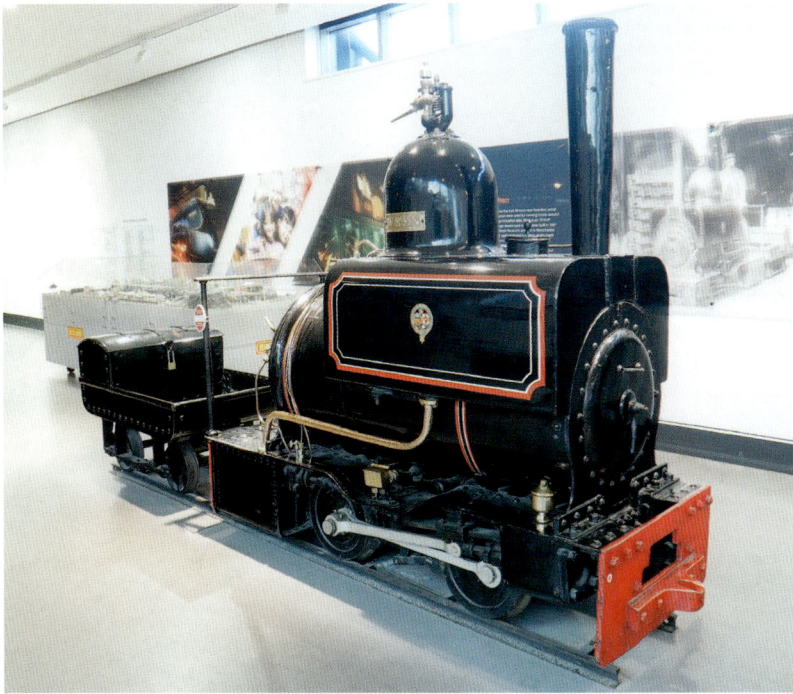

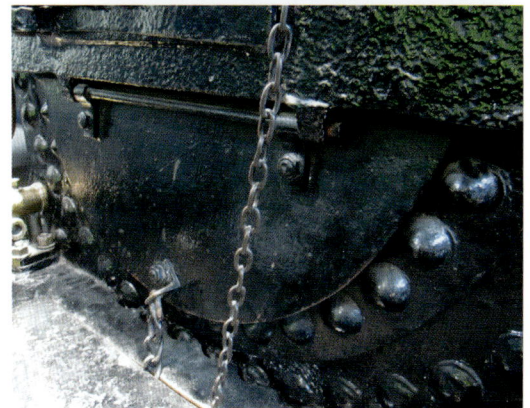

Above left: Crewe was not the only railway works to employ an 18 in gauge railway within its confines. The Lancashire & Yorkshire Railway had a relatively long-lived system around its Horwich works in Lancashire, one steam locomotive from which survives. This is WREN, built in 1887 (works number 2825) and withdrawn in 1963. It was built by Beyer Peacock in Gorton, Manchester, initially without the saddle tank. The design has clear lineage from the Crewe locomotives, and features of interest in our study of SAMSON.

Above right: A close up view of WREN's footplate. It is indicative of the design forced upon the builder by the restricted dimensions of the boiler barrel, firebox and need to fit gauge glasses and filling plugs etc. onto the backhead.

Right: Moving even closer, the damper door arrangement on WREN is revealed in all of its simplicity. A very similar arrangement has been fitted to SAMSON.

the Crewe species, which therefore might be considered the 'Adam and Eve' of successful 'compact' narrow gauge locomotive design and whose manifestation in forms long after its first appearance in Cheshire demonstrated its soundness for the specific application for which it was created – namely lightweight loads, short distances and for occasional bursts of activity rather than sustained running. The pay-off was economy and simplicity.

It is also worth noting some significant examples of the 'traction engine locomotive' design built, principally by Aveling & Porter of Rochester and John Fowler in Leeds, some examples of which were seen on page 27. SAMSON (and later HOPS, MALT and LINDHOLME which all followed later) are what might be more accurately termed an 'overtype' locomotive, i.e. one where the cylinder (or cylinders) is positioned on top of the boiler in what was to become the almost universal style employed on traction engines and steam rollers. The engine unit comprises the cylinder, slide bars, piston, connecting

rod and crankshaft plus associated components for the Stephenson valve gear.

The drive from the crankshaft was then taken to the rail-wheels via gears or chain, and in turn these wheels might or might not be coupled by conventional coupling rods or chain, if coupled at all. Aveling produced by far the most examples, the design enduring across six decades and evolving into more sophisticated designs including locomotives with compound cylinders – these having two bores in a block, with the steam used twice, first in a smaller high pressure bore then passing into a larger lower pressure bore to increase power and efficiency.

Five examples of the Aveling design have been preserved and a further derelict narrow gauge example is now kept in a museum. No Fowler examples, the next largest producer of traction engine locomotives, have survived.

Above left: Another works locomotive is DOT, *this time built by Beyer Peacock for use on their own internal railway system at the same time that they were building near-identical locomotives for the L&Y. Built in 1887 (works number 2817), it was retired and presented to the Narrow Gauge Railway Museum at Tywyn in 1961,* DOT *has all of those features seen on* WREN, *with the exception of the saddle tank. The neat firehole door surround and casting is seen in detail here.*

Abnove right: A close look inside DOT's *firebox, which is still complete with firebars and the firebrick/cement bridge which gives space for combustion and keeps the tube nest free of debris from the fire which would otherwise soon clog this area up. This is a situation that Beamish's replica* PUFFING BILLY *shares but without the brick bridge and so great care has to be taken when firing not to throw coal forward into this space which will greatly inhibit the engine's ability to draw the fire and produce steam.*

Left and below: Not referred to in the main text, but of interest because of the non-depending firebox design, are the unique locomotives designed by Samuel Geoghagan for the Guinness Brewery tramways, where he was the Chief Engineer. Frustrated by the inadequacies of locomotives purchased from manufacturers such as Sharp, Stewart and Stephen Lewin for use on the 1 ft 10 in gauge railway system, he designed his own and focussed on flexibility and ease of maintenance (but presumably adopted the satisfactory features of Nos.1 – 5). As a result, these locomotives incorporated the non-depending firebox design discussed in this chapter. They could also be placed into a transporter wagon, which effectively converted them to 5 ft 3 in – the Irish standard gauge.

WHERE WAS 'THAT' PHOTOGRAPH TAKEN?

That only one image of SAMSON at Cornish Hush is known about is, perhaps, unfortunate – although this is balanced by the level of information that this very clear photograph reveals. The side view proved to be invaluable in scaling the locomotive for drawings to be produced, and its positioning in front of a substantial stone building gave key clues as to the location where it was taken. The building is a stone two/three-storey structure with a single storey extension of similar though newer construction, given the bright lime mortar that can clearly be seen. The roof is also stone and the original structure, which we can reasonably presume is the mine shop (workshop) may also house miners on the top floor. The purpose of the extension is not clear, but it may be an engine shed or stables?

Behind the building is a steep hillside and in the foreground are the lines that SAMSON is stood on with sidings just visible behind (to the surmised engine shed?) and to the right approaching the photographer. In Chapter 1 the possible remains of the rear wall of this building at first floor level were indicated. For the map reference, the very much more precise coordinates of NY99859,33424 can be given for the centreline of the roof of the building shown on the 1894 survey.

Left: The author and David compare the photograph with the site of the building marked on the map. There is certainly space for all of the features shown, the alignment of the building and the logical arrangement of sidings from the mine also fit the hypothesis, and the hillside behind is similar, allowing for inevitable changes in vegetation.

Below: Satisfied that the location of the original photograph has been identified, David joins the group photo, over 130 years late for the moment described in the introduction of this book!

CHAPTER 5

NARROW GAUGE STEAM LOCOMOTIVES IN THE DURHAM DALES LEAD MINING INDUSTRY

Above: No.1 is seen working on the tramway at Groove Rake, complete with the very neat iron bodied tubs used at this location. The bunker appears to be struggling to contain a particularly large lump of coal which has been jammed into the top of it. As well as snow lying on the ground, the mine's tips are also evident in the background.

AMSON WAS NOT THE ONLY narrow gauge steam locomotive to live out a relatively obscure life in the dales of the River Wear hinterland. Two more locomotives, of more conventional appearance, also saw out their entire working existence in the pursuit of lead, and in doing so draw the modern industrial archaeologist's attention to three fascinating narrow gauge tramways.

The Weardale Lead Company Ltd was formed in 1883, with the primary objective of obtaining the ore extraction leases previously owned by the Beaumont family (who traded as W. B. Lead) and who, when faced with the decline of the industry in the late 19th century, surrendered their interests, the new investors largely originating from the London financial markets.

The company operated various narrow gauge tramways to serve its operations, connecting mines with processing mills and smelters

Right: This view of Wolfcleugh is looking westwards along the valley with Groove Rake mine in the distance. The headgear is clearly visible here, similarly the iron bodied waggons used on this tramway. LITTLE SALLY can just be discerned to the left of the headgear, whilst the winding engine house is to the right of it. The tramway can be seen on the left hand side, climbing steeply towards the photographer on its run eastwards towards Rispey Mill.

Below: This is the only known photograph of No.1 on the tramway at Stanhopeburn. This view was taken around 1914 and shows the cab back has been removed and a wooden ledge fitted atop the remains of the backsheet. One other known photograph of the locomotive working at Wolfcleugh shows that it was fitted with wooden doors on the cab, to shield the driver from at that exposed location – clearly no such luxury was felt to be needed just a few miles to the east! The tramway at Stanhopeburn is rather more sheltered however. Also of note are the inside frame skip wagons (these have a loose body that can tip to either side in order to discharge their load, whilst the wheeled chassis remains on the track – usually!). The file note for this image at Beamish mentions three names: R. Foster, W. Bainbridge and Isaac Gowland – the latter being the post boy.

Right: As the caption on this image makes clear, this is the dressing floor at Stanhopeburn Mine, looking up the valley towards the north, the smelt mill in the distance. The tramway can be seen in the foreground with the 'skip' waggons to the left where they are being loaded. This area was later extensively altered, not least in connection with the 1970s SAMUK operations on the site which saw the original blacksmiths shop converted into a (battery-electric) locomotive shed, which remains today, though was not associated with LITTLE SALLY, which was stabled at the other end of the tramway. This building is just visible directly above the skip waggons. Also of note are the London Lead Company type bottom discharge waggons, which presumably were being used to bring ore to the surface from the adjacent adit, to the left of the blacksmiths shop.

The tramway itself followed the route of a standard gauge Waggonway and the wider formation pictured here in this sylvan scene reveals the spacious trackbed for the 2ft 6 track laid in 1906 by the Weardale Lead Company. This route remains unchanged today and like the Cornish Hush Tramway, seems to beg for a narrow gauge railway to be re-laid along its course once again…

STANHOPEBURN MINE DRESSING FLOORS

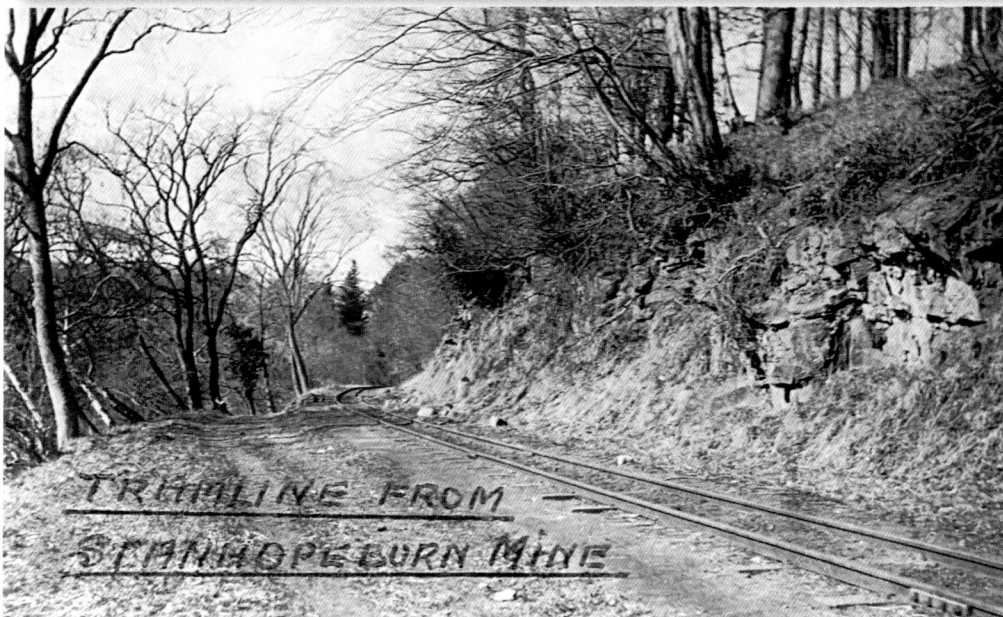

TRAMLINE FROM STANHOPEBURN MINE

in order to carry the bulkier ore in large enough volumes to make the business economically viable. Their first tramway to modernise from horse to steam power was that connecting Groove Rake (later Groverake) mine (NY896442 – some three miles to the west of the village of Rookhope – with Rispey Mill to the east, over a mile downstream on the Rookhope Burn.

This tramway was built in the 1880s, when lead mining resumed at Groove Rake following nearly two decades dormancy. In 1889 Black Hawthorn of Gateshead supplied a 0-4-0ST (Saddle Tank), works No.981 but locally known as No.1, to work the tramway. With 5 in x 10 in cylinders, the locomotive was gauged for the 2 ft 6 in

tramway and settled down as the sole mechanised motive power the tramway ever utilised.

In 1901 Wolfcleugh Mine (NY902432), lying between Groove Rake and Rispey Mill, was re-opened and connected to the tramway, precipitating the closure of the mine at Groove Rake but not the tramway, possibly as despite the cessation of operations there, the latter offered a connection with the standard gauge extension of the Weatherhill & Rookhope Railway (built by the Weardale Iron Company).

For No.1, its working life on the tramway ended in 1909, leaving horses to continue in its place as late as 1930, but it now began a

Dressed in Sunday Best, Ralph Walton (left) and Tom Woodhall appear to have borrowed a waggon in order to transport their companions up or down the Stanhopeburn tramway. The waggon has clearly seen better days, its end door missing. Other photographs show iron bodied skip waggons in use at this location, so perhaps this is a relic from the London Lead Company or even W. B. Lead Company days?

new association with another tramway, whose route is still clearly visible today.

In 1866 W. B. Lead took over the Stanhopeburn Mine (NY986413) from the London Lead Company, which included a standard gauge railway connecting the mine (and Stanhope Smelt Mill a little further north west along the Stanhopeburn) to the North Eastern Railway (formerly the Stanhope & Tyne Railway, amongst others) near the base of the Crawleyside Incline. The mine soon closed and the railway was lifted, but in 1906 it was reopened by the Weardale Lead Company for the extraction of fluorspar and the tramway reinstated, this time to 2 ft 6 in gauge, with an interchange to sidings at Lanehead Quarry (now owned by the Consett Iron Company) and whence to the North Eastern Railway via the Crawleyside Incline.

The tramway was horse worked to begin with, but in 1909 the Hudswell Clarke from Wolfcleugh was transferred to this new tramway, by now having gained the name LITTLE SALLY. The mine closed in 1933, three years after production was suspended, so it may

be assumed that LITTLE SALLY was also out of use at that time, later being scrapped in 1937, probably when the mine was reopened again under yet another owner. At some point during the locomotive's working life, it was rebuilt by Hawthorn Leslie, who attached their works No. 4109 to this well-proportioned and pretty little engine.

The third tramway in the Weardale Lead Company portfolio of interest here was that used at Boltsburn Mine adjacent to the village of Rookhope (NY936428). Totalling around 1¼ miles in length, the tramway connected the mine with the smelting mill to the west and the washing mill to the south east. The arrival of the Weatherhill & Rookhope Railway (standard gauge) in latter half of the 1840s brought great change to the transport topography of the area, intersecting the tramway at all three of its destinations.

Presumed to have been built to 2 ft 6 in gauge, the whole route was rebuilt in 1913 with the arrival of LITTLE NUT, built by R & W Hawthorn Leslie & Co, Newcastle (works No.3029) and fitted with 5 in x 10 in cylinders. Given the number '2' it was of similar design to No.1 LITTLE SALLY but was built to run on 1 ft 10 in gauge. It

The
Little NUT
(N⁰2).

Above: This view of No.2 LITTLE NUT, taken from a captioned postcard and probably captured shortly after arrival at Boltsburn Mine reveals the unusual emphasis on the 'NUT' in the locomotive's name. It also sports the semi-open cab and appears very much as it does in a works photograph taken in 1913.

Right: Still in excellent external condition, No.2 has now had an enclosed cab fitted, with cosmetic appeal clearly playing second fiddle to practicality! The Giffard injector is prominently visible underneath the saddle tank, the trimming wheel favoured on this make marking it out from other injector designs.

Right: An overview of the mine at Boltsburn with the boilerhouse in the background within the larger of the two buildings on the left and an enclosed waterwheel (used to power the mine's pumps) in the tall structure dominating the right hand cluster of buildings. The enclosure of the waterwheel gave a degree of protection from the weather, particularly power loss due to high winds or freezing of water on the wheel itself. The steam was used to drive air compressors as well as supply the winding engine on site. The waggons (or 'tubs') are aligned on two roads (for empties and fulls?) adjacent to the mine's headgear and from here they would be worked to the crusher and smelter as required.

Below: A rake of bottom discharge tubs at Boltsburn. The waggons used by the London Lead Company are described in a later chapter, but there is very much a family resemblance between the two company's rolling stock. These examples differ in that the frames are longer and the buffing forces pass through the chassis (rather than the body of non-locomotive worked waggons), appear to be longer and have a different arrangement for the side frames. This photograph is believed to date from around 1910, so it pre-dates the arrival of LITTLE NUT *on the tramway here.*

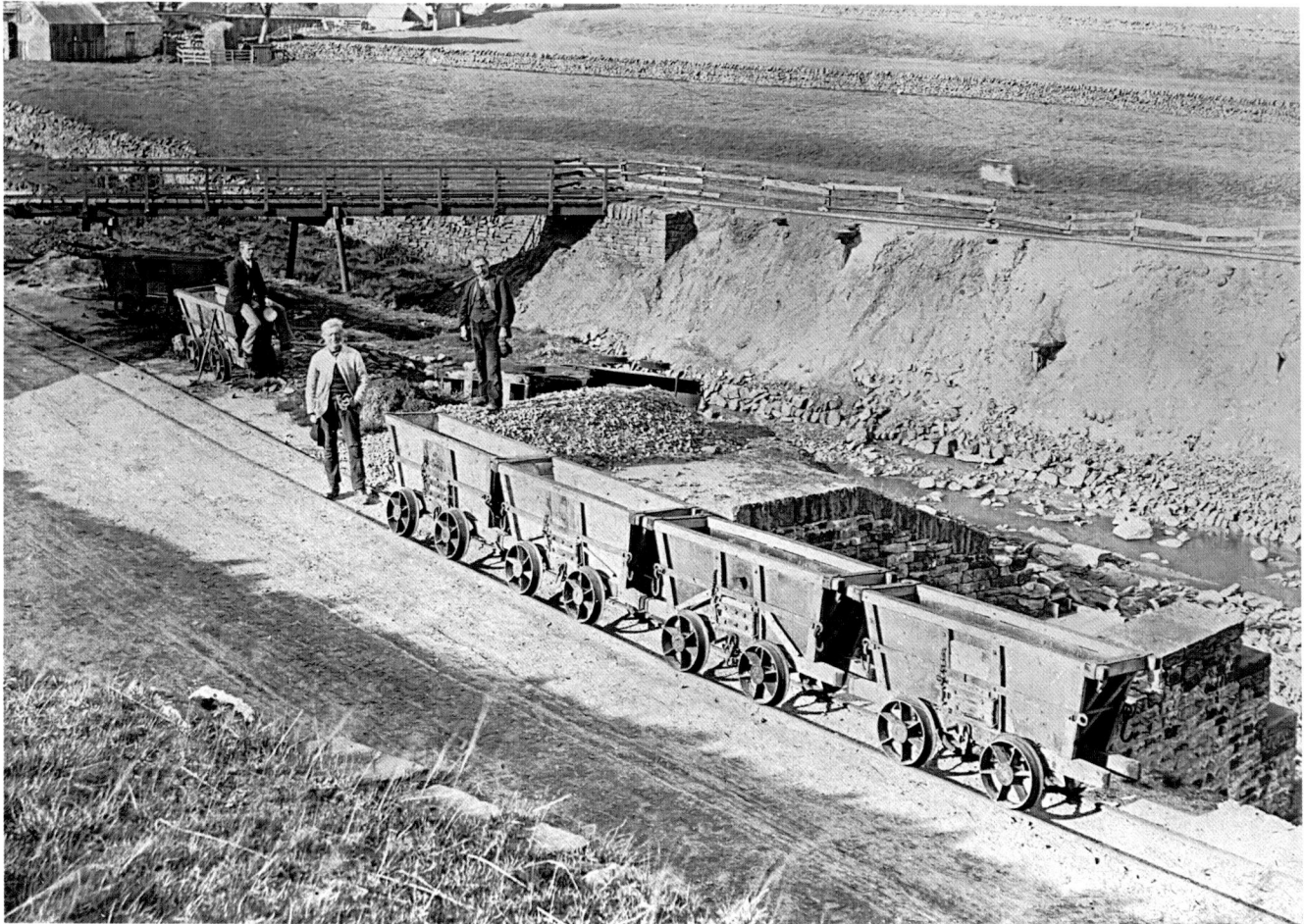

The replica Boltsburn tramway snowplough, as propelled by No.2 LITTLE NUT, at Beamish in appropriate weather conditions.

has been speculated that it was a cancelled export order and that the Weardale Lead Company took advantage of a cheaply available locomotive, finding it more expeditious to re-gauge the tramway rather than the engine! The name has also been explained by the small stature and initials of its place of construction in Newcastle upon Tyne, an alternative that it was originally destined for Brazil. Whether such tales have any basis in fact or are entirely apocryphal should not be allowed to stand in the way of fascinating local folklore!

LITTLE NUT was photographed a number of times, revealing that it was later fitted with a locally made enclosed cab in place of the open original (further weight to the idea of it being intended for export?). It was provided with a corrugated iron single road engine shed at the mine and, unusually, a snowplough, this being mounted on four wheels with a substantial body (to enable ballasting with waste stone) made of timber boards and fitted with an iron two-sided ploughing blade. A photograph of the plough (and engine shed) survives, and the remains of the plough were later moved to Beamish where a replica of this wonderful relic was constructed and

can be seen today. The engine itself was out of use from 1919 when the smelting mill was closed, being scrapped around 1934.

Further study of these fascinating tramways and the industry they made viable must start with the monumental volume *The Industrial Railways & Locomotives of County Durham* – Part 1 by Colin E. Mountford and Dave Holroyde and published by the Industrial Railway Society in 2006. This has been a key source of information on No.1 and No.2 plus the tramways that they were associated with. In conjunction with this book, study of the website 'Keys to the Past' (search for this title via Google) and use of the searchable database of locations and maps is highly recommended.

Little Nut

Watercolour by Jonathan Clay

Jonathan Clay 2007

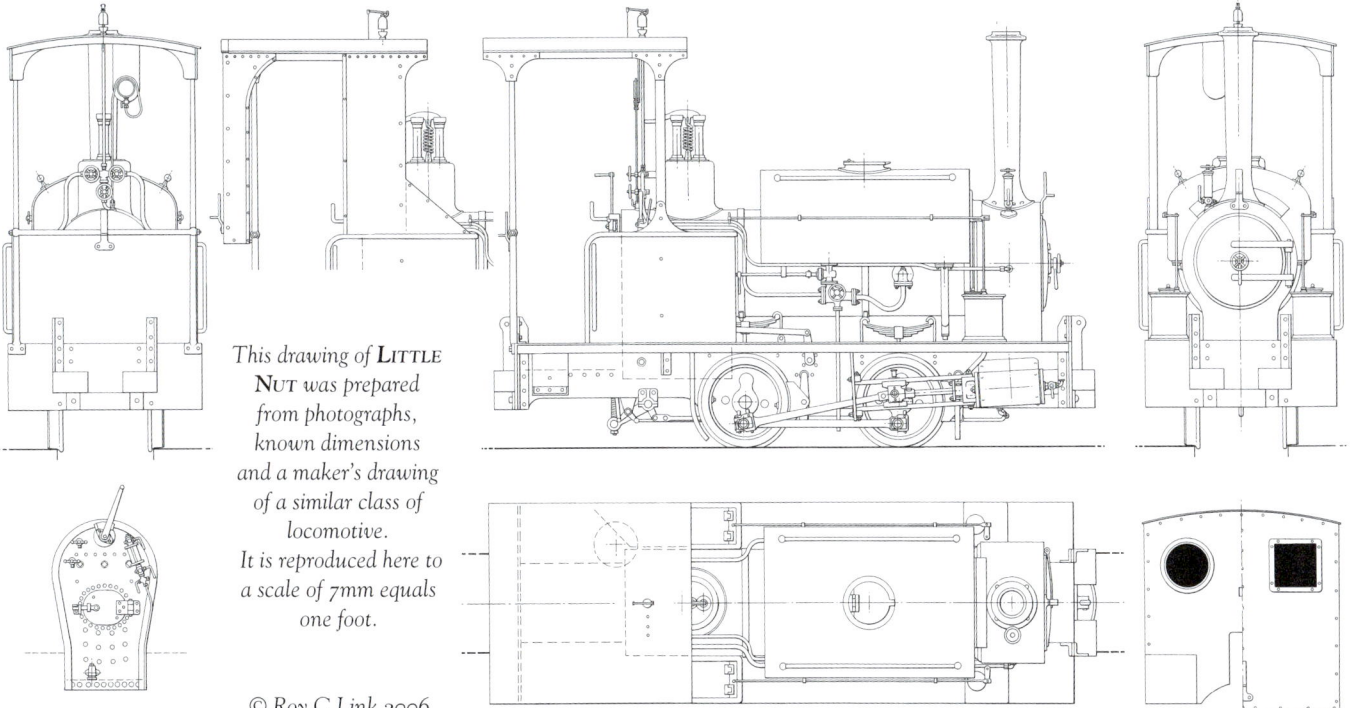

This drawing of **Little Nut** was prepared from photographs, known dimensions and a maker's drawing of a similar class of locomotive.
It is reproduced here to a scale of 7mm equals one foot.

© Roy C Link 2006

CHAPTER 6
SAMSON REBORN

Jonathan Clay 2013

Many a new locomotive construction or restoration project has begun with the commissioning of a painting of the chosen subject from renowned railway artist Jonathan Clay. SAMSON was no exception (in fact, at Beamish there are over 20 paintings of transport subjects created by Jonathan!), an added challenge being the author's request for a front three quarter view – a view not known of the original locomotive and therefore pieced together based on David's drawings and other Stephen Lewin locomotives which were less shy in revealing their smokebox faces!

BEFORE DESCRIBING THE CREATION of the second SAMSON, some background history to the last decade of locomotive restoration and creation at Beamish may be of interest to the reader. The Museum had first fraternised with the 'new-build' concept when it became associated with Mike Satow and Locomotion Enterprises in the mid-1970s. The objective was the construction of a replica of the Stockton & Darlington Railway LOCOMOTION No.1 for the 1975 S&DR 150th anniversary celebrations at Shildon, County Durham (home of the extensive wagon works and therefore ideally suited to hosting what became an iconic event). Once the celebrations were over, LOCOMOTION was moved to Beamish where it took up residence and remains today (though it was extensively rebuilt in 1995 and again awaits such work to replace the boiler in 2016).

Moments along the road of the construction programme gave particular cause for pleasure. The placing of the boiler barrel atop the frames, with bunkers in place and the wheel castings leant against this assemblage gave some sense of the size of this engine and also reassured doubters that it was not only plausible, but happening!

LOCOMOTION was used for occasional passenger rides and operated out of a shed hastily assembled in the Museum's recreated colliery. In the 1990s an idea was developing which would see the creation of the Pockerley Steam Waggonway on the eastern side of the Museum, a significant feature in a wider Georgian landscape. LOCOMOTION was therefore substantially rebuilt; a train of appropriate rolling stock constructed and, thanks to its forays to Japan for various world trade fairs, significant investment was available from the engine's earnings to construct the impressive engine shed/works from which the Waggonway operation would be based.

This much enhanced operation (running daily through the summer season) gave rise to the construction of a second new-build, this time based on a locomotive which had originated in 1815, assembled by John Buddle and William Chapman from parts made at the Hawks foundry in Gateshead for use on the Wallsend Waggonway to the east of Newcastle-upon-Tyne. Based on a contemporary oil painting and some documentary evidence, STEAM ELEPHANT was completed in 2001 and entered service alongside LOCOMOTION.

The next new-build was a replica of the Wylam Waggonway locomotive PUFFING BILLY, the original surviving in the Science Museum in London and therefore enabling a replica to be made based on this, rather than more nebulous information or documentary sources, as had been the case for STEAM ELEPHANT and would be the case for SAMSON. The Waggonway trio was completed in 2006, so it would be another 11 years before another reconstruction to fill a missing 'gap' in regional locomotive history was to enter service at Beamish.

In late 2006 a chance meeting of David Young and the author started what was to become a very fruitful relationship for Beamish. David was engaged in research into one of his former employers, the Washington Chemical Company, making use of the extensive archives at the Museum. The author's recollection is that he was passing through the reception area carrying the very tired regulator quadrant from the Museum's 1871 built Head Wrightson vertical boilered locomotive (usually known as 'COFFEE POT No.1) when it caught the eye of David, who was also passing through at the same time. This resulted in a conversation and the offer of assistance with the restoration of No.1, which was in the early stages, funded by a Heritage Lottery Fund grant. Looking back at the restoration diary for COFFEE POT (available at www.beamishtransportonline. co.uk on the last page of the 'News' section) reveals just how quickly

Another moment of great satisfaction came at Christmas 2015 when SAMSON's assembly was completed as far as was possible ahead of the first steam testing. The aluminium paint applied to the boiler has a certain appeal, though would be hidden later once the lagging and cladding was fitted. The gear-guard in particular captures the character of the locomotive, for so long gazed at in two engravings and a single photograph. Here it was for all to see in the flesh once again

COFFEE POT No.1 *sometime between 1871 (when it was built) and 1874, when it was first re-boilered (it developing something of an appetite for boilers thereafter, probably due to their less than satisfactory condition as they were purchased second-hand).*

David became associated with the project and how he enabled what was going to be an overhaul of the existing locomotive around the construction of a new boiler to become a comprehensive restoration, complete with the recreation of many of the original fittings and making full use of his pattern making abilities, foundry contacts and skills machining the various sub-assemblies.

Without a doubt that chance meeting enabled No.1's restoration, completed at Easter 2010, to attain a far higher standard than would otherwise have been possible. It might be seen as unprofessional for the author in his role at Beamish to have a favourite object amongst the many thousands that fall within his responsibility, but No.1 would certainly top the list, not just as a machine, but for the enjoyable and instructive process by which its rebirth into its 1870s guise came about and a lasting friendship with David was struck.

With No.1 reaching completion attention was then turned to the next project. No.18, the 1877 built Stephen Lewin locomotive that worked for 89 years at Seaham Harbour, was very much the next favoured and a detailed 'archaeological' assessement had

FUNDING THE NEW SAMSON

It is perhaps worth adding a few words regarding funding to the narrative at this point. Looking back across the project, and adding in David's contribution in hours (at a very conservative rate of £30 per hour equivalent value), it soon reveals the cost to be not insubstantial, even for a very small locomotive. When the project started, it was known that the labour would largely be given voluntarily, from both David and the author. Time sheets were kept and reveal an equivalent labour cost somewhere in the region of £110,000 in value – a very substantial input into not only the project but the Museum as a whole.

The boiler design, carried out by Graham Morris, and the PED (Pressure Equipment Directive) application, plus fees for the notified body for insurance approval of the design (through to final testing and CE marking for conformity) carried out by British Engineering Services (formerly Royal Sun Alliance) totalled roughly £3000.

The material for the frames, coupling rods, buffer beams and crankshaft (including profiling them precisely to shape) was given to the project as a gift, so saving in the region of £3000. Further to this was a financial donation from Alan Moore, a supporter of railway preservation nationally and a previous generous supporter of steam locomotive projects at Beamish. This covered the costs of the boiler plates required for the tubeplates, firebox and backhead (including forming). This equated to an additional £6000.

A tremendous boost to the project was received when Graham Lee agreed to assemble the wheelsets. This entailed using supplied castings, which his Statfold Barn workshops machined, fitted tyres to, pressed on to axles and then fitted crankpins to the peculiar asymmetrical design required to accommodate the gear rings. This work had not been costed when his offer was received but would undoubtedly have added as much as £10,000 to the bill as well as considerable time in procurement and management of the work.

Other contracts such as gear cutting and specialist machining work were carried out at favourable rates, and, including assembly of the boiler (which was carried out at Bridgnorth on the Severn Valley Railway and received a large degree of labour input from Beamish staff) then the equivalent of £8000 can be added to the bill. Castings, materials, paint, nuts and bolts, rivets and miscellaneous items including backhead fittings, injector and valves (most of which were paid for by donations or from articles the author had written for the specialist press) added a further £8000. A final consideration is the staff time commitment at Beamish. This includes the author (though most of this commitment was done outside of work hours as a voluntary contribution, including painting the locomotive and is not included in the final total) and Chris Armstrong, the RHEC Engineering Technician who carried out much of the welding and fabrication jobs required and who worked closely with David whenever this work was required. If factored as a staff cost, this contribution would add a further £2000 or so to the sum total.

This brings the grand total cost, if it had been procured entirely on a commercial basis, to approximately £150,000. Allowing for many hours spent by the those involved simply thinking about the project, considering options and solving problems, a sum of around £150,000 - £160,000 would not be an unreasonable amount to put against the project if a new SAMSON was to be purchased off the shelf. The cost to Beamish in cash terms was very small, but the value as a contribution to the new exhibit was clearly substantial and equally reflected the very same process that had been applied to No.1 and No.18 and to some extent the STEAM MULE and which is probably entirely recognisable to restorers and creators of steam engines across the land.

commenced, with David Potter carrying out a comprehensive survey to produce a fully drawn record of what survived. This was particularly important for its restoration, also recording what was needed to recreate its 1936 guise (the point in its history at which it could be backdated to without losing any quantity of original material). The restoration work was extensive and virtually everything above the running plates (including most of the running plates themselves) is of new construction. Again David immersed himself almost full-time into this ambitious project and the list of his accomplishments on this locomotive's restoration would fill a book of its own (and maybe will one day...).

Alongside No.18's restoration, a small new-build, and the first to carry a Beamish works number (BM1) was created. A small vertical steam boiler of modern manufacture but traditional style had been donated by Tyne & Wear Archives and Museums and this seemed too good not to utilise. The author's fondness for the 'unusual' re-awakened a memory of the small portable engines sometimes created by local agricultural engineers (and exemplified by a preserved example illustrated here) and the need for a suitable means of training steam engine operators for the Museum, from a novice starting point, combined to create the STEAM MULE.

As No.18's restoration to steam drew to a close, discussions began as to what might be tackled next. The Museum's priorities had developed over the duration of the previous projects and had seen the purchase of an 1895 built 0-4-4T named DUNROBIN which had been supplied to the 4th Duke of Sutherland for hauling his private saloon coach over the Highland Railway between Inverness and Dunrobin Castle, a railway which his father had financed in part as a shareholder of the Highland Railway and in part directly after the former was unable to complete the construction northwards towards Golspie. A complication was that the engine (and saloon) were located in Canada where they had resided since 1965.

Seaham Harbour Dock Company No.18
The only surviving Stephen Lewin built locomotive is one which is actually more accurately described as a Seaham Harbour built engine utilising substantial components from an earlier Stephen Lewin engine. The story begins in 1877 when works number 683 was supplied to the Londonderry Railway for use at Seaham Harbour as their No.18. Built as a well-tank locomotive, its appearance was substantially different to that in which it would later gain a certain amount of fame amongst railway enthusiasts (see below). In 1936 the harbour engineers, by now working for the Seaham Harbour Dock Company, turned out a rebuilt No.18. Fitted with a revised cab, a saddle tank and with the frames substantially altered to remove the well-tanks and incorporate additional frame stretchers, it is also likely that at this point the boiler was renewed. The cab was modified in 1960 during an overhaul, but otherwise the locomotive remained largely unaltered as it ran for another 33 years, its eventual withdrawal coming in 1969 when the boiler was condemned (see upper left).

Their repatriation and restoration for use at Beamish reflected a resurgence in the role of railways at the Museum and a step change in scale as intensive restorations/rebuilds were now being tackled in order to enable regular operation of the various railways across the site. This entailed extensive use of contractors and inevitably altered the focus for funding and project management. Nevertheless, a small project of modest proportion was both desirable and possible, particularly as the newly opened Regional Heritage Engineering Centre (RHEC) offered much improved facilities for engineering on site.

Both David and the author had both been drawn to the Stephen Lewin locomotive SAMSON, immortalised for those who sought it out in all of its obscurity, by the single photograph of it at Cornish Hush. Some discussion took place regarding construction of a large

scale model of SAMSON, bolstered by the knowledge that renowned model engineer Ken Swan (based at Beamish as part of the model engineering group there) had considered such a venture, on 7¼in gauge, in the 1980s. He had ruled it out as having insufficient information to support such a project and had embarked upon his well-known Kerr Stuart Wren and Orenstein & Koppel rack locomotive designs.

However, the effort to build SAMSON in miniature did not seem to fall far short of that required to build it in full size, in fact, ever so slightly larger to account for the 2 in gauge increase needed to enable operation on the narrow gauge railway at Beamish. The author was also keen for the RHEC to prove its new capabilities and what better way than by constructing a new, full-size (admittedly of a small prototype!) steam locomotive?

The completed STEAM MULE with a proud David stood beside it. The boiler had not required any significant attention and was installed directly onto the trolley once this was completed.

Above: No.18 and No.1 are seen together at Beamish – at 139 and 145 years old respectively, and working with waggons dating from the 1870s, this is a unique scene that can only be recreated at the Museum and is one which SAMSON will join, running on the adjacent narrow gauge railway system.

With the momentum building, David set about producing drawings (another of his skills emerging from his training and early working career as a draughtsman at Washington Chemical Company). It was loosely agreed that a number of patterns would be made to enable the more complex components to be manufactured, and if successful, then the project would be considered viable, though it is almost certain that all doubts regarding viability had already been dispelled in the minds of the two protagonists!

On 18 April 2012, the author placed a post on the Beamish Transport Blog which indicated his intentions without giving the game away regarding what was being planned. The post read:

The image below [the view of SAMSON at Cornish Hush] shows a delightful little locomotive named SAMSON. It was built by the Poole Foundry of Stephen Lewin in 1874 and was for a long time thought to be the first railway locomotive that they built. There is now some doubt about this fact, but regardless of this, it is certainly an early railway product for the firm.

It was supplied new to the London Lead Company's Cornish Hush leadmine, Whitfield Brow near Frosterley. Often erroneously stated as working in Middleton-in-Teesdale (where the firm actually had its headquarters) the engine operated over a mile long tramway between the mine and the crushing plant. The mine leases were surrendered in 1883 and the 1898 OS map for the area (second edition) shows the crushing mill closed and the tramway abandoned. The London Lead Company was wound up in 1905. It seems that the locomotive itself was sold, presumably for scrap, and removed via the NER's Middleton-in-Teesdale station in 1904, suggesting it had been removed to the headquarters for storage after the tramway closed.

The engine therefore enjoyed only a short working life. It is of particular note because of its unusual design, being an 'overtype' with crankshaft and flywheel drive. This is very much along traction engine or portable engine lines. Lewins built other engines to this pattern (notably 'Hops' and 'Malt' for the Guinness brewery) but it was not a common practice in railway locomotive design.

Samson was 1 ft 10 in gauge and of very tiny proportions, as can be seen here. It was said to weigh 2 tons 12 cwt and attracted some interest in the contemporary technical press, resulting in two engravings being produced showing it, though the detail accuracy of these must be doubted in some regards. However, unlike some of the other smaller Lewin locomotives, which were fitted with marine type fireboxes, this engine appears to have a locomotive boiler. The far side (not shown in the photograph) would appear to have external gears on the wheels (front and rear), connecting with the drive via layshafts off the crankshaft These were enclosed for safety.

Samson would certainly make an interesting subject for replication for use on our new narrow gauge railway…

The result was some interesting discussion, with suggestions of alternative locomotives that might be suitable for 'our new narrow gauge railway'. In fact, another potential candidate was the R. W. Hawthorn 0-4-0ST Little Nut which operated on the 22 in gauge tramway at Boltsburn Mine and described elsewhere. It was felt that the costs of building this would be too high, largely due to the work required to create the larger and more complex boiler design, but in hindsight it would probably have been a viable project albeit costlier and more time consuming.

The initial blog posting was followed up with a look at the Cornish Hush Tramway, but then on 11 January 2013 a posting was placed titled 'Introducing Samson – a new project for the New Year'. Accompanied by a selection of photographs showing completed patterns for the cylinder block components, flywheel and crankshaft pedestals (to demonstrate that it was very much a running project and not a pipe-dream), the author wrote:

Having dropped numerous hints over a number of previous blog postings, I can now confirm that our 'new build' steam locomotive project is the Stephen Lewin 0-4-0WTG Samson, the original originating from 1874 and scrapped, it is thought, sometime around 1904.

The rationale was explored thus:

Dave and I looked at the potential of the project as something ideal for our new Regional Heritage Engineering Centre to build – a great way to put the facility on the map and also a project on which apprentices, staff and volunteers could learn, train and hone skills on. Being a small engine, space would not be too much of an issue, nor handling of even the more substantial components. However, it does require a professional approach as well and so the management will be per our Safety Management System for such work and some specialist services will be needed, such as finalising the boiler design etc.

One thing needed, with any new-build announcement, is credibility. Therefore, to prove the project was feasible, David prepared the drawings for the project and then made the most complicated patterns, for the cylinder block. This gave us confidence and so he continued to produce detail drawings as well as patterns at a furious rate. Meanwhile, I arranged to have the frames, crankshaft and several other components profile cut at no cost to the Museum in order that when we went public (i.e. this post!) we could show we had a feasible project, patterns to hand and a set of frames upon which to build as well as the workshops in which to do it. Happy that this stage has been demonstrated, the project is thus announced and tangible progress can already be demonstrated.

The concluding paragraphs ran:

One question the reader is bound to have is 'how long will this take and what will it cost?' Timescales are always tricky but Dave and I would like to think we could have something resembling Samson and working, under steam, within three years, maybe sooner. Of course, this depends on finance and I am conscious that in these straightened times, and with a major capital programme looming for Beamish, the Samson project must be carried out as expeditiously as possible – it must be cheap but not create a cheap result! Dave's considerable input, the use of our own workshop facilities, my own time as project manager and the soliciting of free work and materials all thus contribute to this to the point that I think at this stage we are able to start and over the next 18 months I will look for further support for the project in order to assist in bringing it to fruition.

So began three years of construction, with David carrying out the majority of the design, drawing and engineering and the author managing the project overall, setting a curatorial direction and managing the various contracts which were required alongside those skills supplied by David. It was intended to do as much as possible of the work within the RHEC at Beamish, but inevitably some work would be carried out elsewhere, not least the assembly of the boiler which had to conform to strict regulations for its assembly and testing. At this point an artist's impression of the finished locomotive was commissioned from transport artist Jonathan Clay – with this hanging on the wall the project had to progress!

CHAPTER 7
CONSTRUCTION IN DETAIL
– FRAMES AND FOOTPLATE

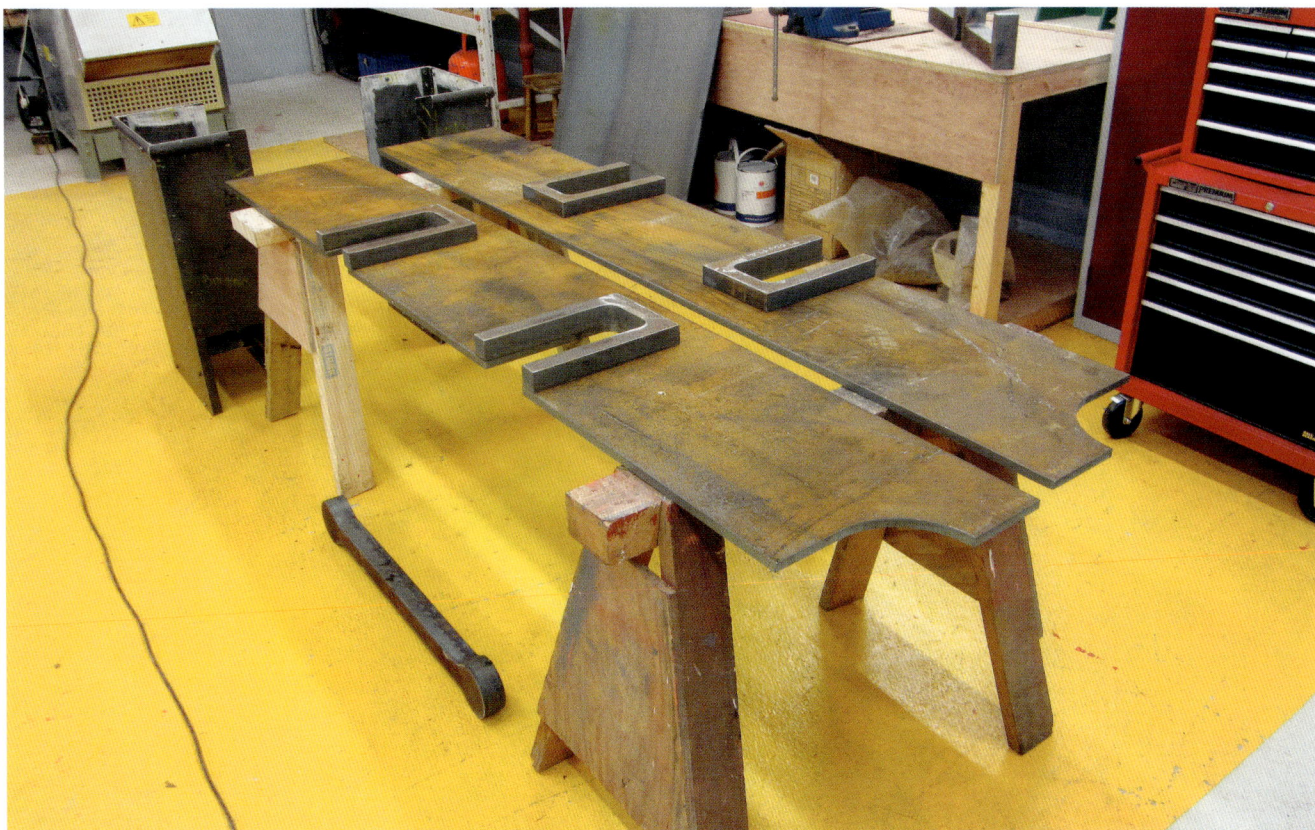

As with all locomotives, the laying down of the frames marks the commencement of construction. The frames for SAMSON were kindly donated, ready profiled, by a supporter in North Yorkshire. They are seen in their raw state, set on trestles and with the hornguide profiles laid on top of their apertures. In designing the new SAMSON, it had been decided to increase the wheel diameter in order to give better clearance above rail top. The wheelbase was also adjusted to balance these changes and allow two equally sized water tanks to be placed between the frames. These changes are apparent when the observer knows to look for them, but are borne out of sound reasoning and the desire to avoid the footplate striking the rails or any other obstruction.

I T IS INTENDED THAT THE OLD ADAGE of 'a picture is worth a thousand words' will largely speak for the construction phases of the new SAMSON, interwoven with extracts taken from the author's transport blog – which give some contemporary observations on the project's progression. The logical place to start is with the frames of a locomotive, and so it was that the frames were the first components to be manufactured and assembled.

The blog entry for February 4th 2013 stated that:

It is always a pleasant experience when Dave Young wanders into the office looking tired and announcing he has something to show me! It means that he has been busy in his workshop, so today's

revelation was a pair of bunkers for SAMSON. We ordered the steel sheet pre-cut (costs nothing to have this done and is very accurate to specification) and Dave has drilled both these and the angles to allow assembly pre-riveting. Also fitted is the rather nice wide

FRAME FOR LOCOMOTIVE SAMSON

The frame drawing, without the boiler or engine unit, reveals just how long the rear overhang on Samson is. The driving wheel diameter was increased to improve the clearance under the footplate and for the brake gear, which as an underslung type was potentially very vulnerable to contact with the ground.

Drawn by D T Young

Left: The frames were assembled using spacer jigs, which would play a part in their structure until the riveting was completed at a later stage. The footplate, bunkers and bufferbeams have also been added at this stage.

Right: Once the frames had been drilled and the stretchers prepared, they were moved to the Severn Valley Railway for riveting in the boiler works at Bridgnorth. Here the expansion brackets that support the firebox end of the boiler are permanently attached.

(and flat) beading. One bunker will be for coal whilst the other will house the injector and associated pipework as well as a toolbox at the top. The production of the frames is progressing with a large set of components being water-jet profiled for us as a gift to the project by a supporter. This also includes the coupling rods and crankshaft, which can then be turned to suit. It is thus anticipated that erection of the frames will progress fairly rapidly and enable us to consider the riveting of these in the spring.

This posting went under the heading 'SAMSON – First components manufactured' and was notable in being illustrated with a view of the assembled bunker – the first bit of SAMSON to exist. The injector was eventually tucked under the firebox on the footplate rather than inside the bunker as will be seen later.

Above left: Steel rivets provide great strength for making permanent assemblies; the purchase they afford as they are hammered and cool into shape being formidable and stronger than can be achieved by bolting plates together. Above right: Rivets were heated in a portable hearth using an oxygen/propane torch to achieve a yellow glow. The rivet is then offered to the hole into which it will be fitted, speed being a necessarily important element of the process.

Right: The rivets were inserted into their holes (the holes being reamed slightly oversize), then an air 'jammer' was placed behind the existing head and activated, whilst the non-domed end is rounded and hammered home using a hand-held air tool, seen in the right of this view. It is fitted with a 'snap' which forms the domed shape of the rivet and works the shoulder of this tightly against the plate.

Left: Some rivets are 'flush' (countersunk) on Samson's frames, and so were dressed after cooling in order that, in this case, the bunkers would fit tightly against the frame plates on the footplate.

Right: Once the frames had returned to Beamish, the two water tanks were fitted, these being identical in capacity and slung between the frames. The circular holes are to allow access to the tanks for future cleaning/repairs, the frames being upside down in this view. A balance pipe connects the two tanks, which are filled from a point just below the smokebox. As a result a tank level indicator is fitted, as otherwise there is no way of determining the level of water inside the tanks.

Below: In order to keep the frame plates parallel, additional cross-ties were welded into position by Beamish's RHEC Technician Chris Armstrong. The brake hanger was also fitted before the frames were shot-blasted and coated in primer.

Below: A portable hearth was once again employed for another element of the superstructure, this time at Beamish and to enable final riveting of the bunkers.

Right: Matt Beddard, another RHEC Technician, and David wrestle with the bunker plates as they are suspended from a gantry crane over the 'dolly' into which hot rivets are placed before being fed into their holes in the bunker plate.

Right: With the hot rivet in place and the plate positioned, the end of the rivet is hammered over, closing tightly as it cools.

Above: Several sub-assemblies were in-hand as the frames were constructed. The brake handle and shaft is clearly shown in the photograph of the original Samson and David was therefore able to accurately replicate this component. This is the vertical brake shaft, set in David's own lathe as the square profiled screw thread is cut. Below left: The various cranks for the brakegear were cut from solid steel and profiled, with the bushes added separately, before boring to fit the shafts. Below right: The completed vertical brake rod, with bronze bush which runs inside the cast pedestal mounted onto the side of the frame extensions. The rod has a forked jaw at its base which pulls onto a crank in order to apply/release the brake.

Right: The casting for the pedestal is seen in this view, complete with the vertical rod in place and the handle assembly trial fitted.

Below: Cast in gunmetal, the axleboxes were 'fitted' within the hornguides. The internal bearing surface has been machined, likewise the thrust face (against which the rear of the wheels act). The assembly was, at this stage, fully circular, though the bottom of the axlebox would later be machined into a 'U' shape to enable the axle to be slid over the journal machined onto the axle.

Above: A great deal of thought was given to the axleboxes and their lubrication, which must allow movement vertically on their external flanks whilst facilitating the rotation of the axles within their centres. Oil lubrication is used and a means of allowing this to enter the bearing (which the machined area within which the axle rotates is named), and be retained to some extent – this being done in the underkeep, a removable component which contains a felt pad and also acts to keep the axle within the axlebox if the locomotive is lifted. There was no indication about how this was achieved on the original SAMSON, so 'conventional' practice was adopted for the new locomotive. Here is the wooden pattern for the axlebox casting.

Above left: The driving wheels on the new SAMSON have cast iron centres, with rolled steel tyres shrunk onto them. The original featured steel gears and as these appear to have been cast integrally with the wheel, it is probable that the wheel and gears were cast as one piece, then machined to finished specification. There were numerous reasons not to replicate this particular feature, tyred wheels being more durable and separate gears easier to manufacture to name two. Here are the patterns for the wheel centres – two were cast first, then the pattern modified to include the spigots to carry the ring gears on the left hand side of the locomotive before the remaining two castings were made. Above right: The wheel centres for the left hand side of SAMSON, revealing their substantial mass as well as the seats to which the ring gear is fitted.

Right: The castings were sent to the Statfold Barn Railway, whose proprietor Graham Lee had generously offered to complete them to finished specification. With the centres turned, tyres fitted, axles machined and fitted and crankpins machined and pressed into the castings, the wheels are seen here after arrival at Beamish and application of several coats of black paint.

The tyre profile was to a recognised narrow gauge profile and the back-to-backs (distance between the backs of the flanged tyres and a critical dimension) was set to 21⅜ ins. This was to give Samson the maximum range of compatibility with narrow gauge railways, where a nominal '2ft' gauge can vary considerably.

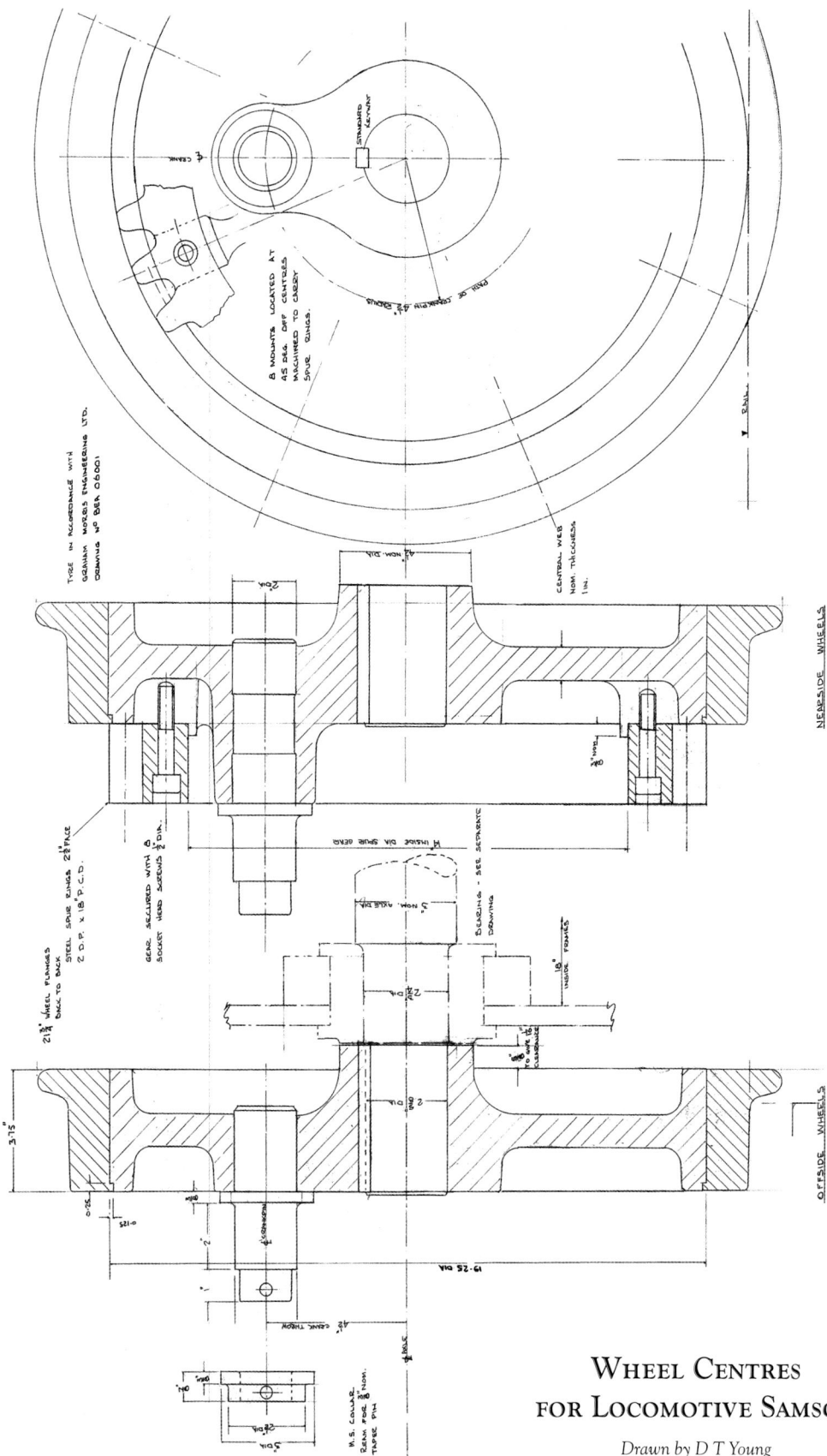

WHEEL CENTRES
FOR LOCOMOTIVE SAMSON

Drawn by D T Young

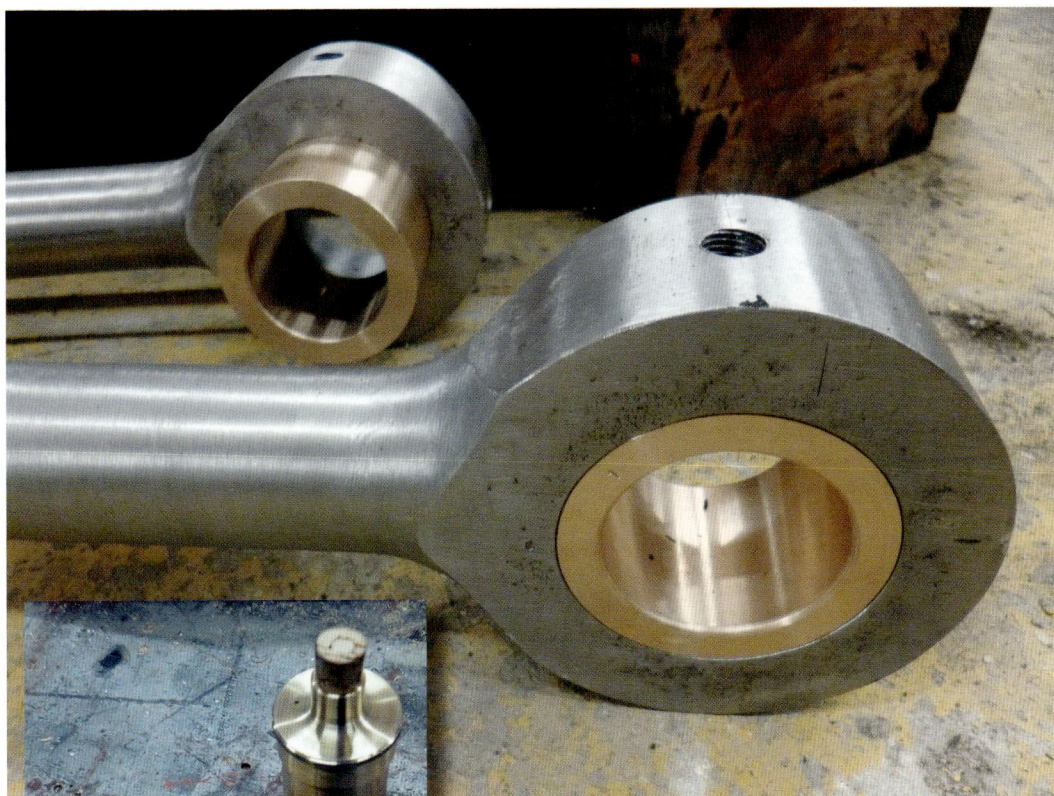

Left: The two coupling rods were supplied with the frame plates as profiled blanks, which were then laboriously machined to a circular 'fishbelly' profile - that is that they are thicker in the middle than at the ends where they flare out to the bearing ends. All of this is one piece. Bronze bushes were then machined and pressed home, the holes at the top of each rod seen here being to enable the fitting of the lubricating pots.

Left: centre: Two of the four coupling rod oil pots, made from gunmetal blanks and with an internal stem into which a wool wick is placed in order to feed a gradual supply of oil to the bearing surface. The caps are removable, but corks are also fitted for ease of filling. These components were made from patterns created during the restoration of No.18, being based on Stephen Lewin practice deduced from photographic evidence.

Right: The original SAMSON did not have anything fitted to the rear of the footplate for the safety or comfort of the crew, something not thought desirable on the new locomotive. Therefore a set of stepped vertical balustrades were made by architectural blacksmith Andrew Basnett, which fit the side frame extensions but enable maximum space on the footplate for the crew. A set of smaller balustrades were also made to hold the footplate at its rear up to the rear bufferbeam. Details like this are important in ensuring the right 'feel' for the new locomotive, the blacksmith's hammer marks being far more appealing than a sterile fabrication.

The vertical supports which give rigidity to the rear footplate and bufferbeam assembly. Seen here before the oak bufferbeams were fitted.

The frames were assembled onto the wheelsets, the coupling rods added and bufferbeams completed. This was to enable some running-in to be carried out whilst the boiler was under construction.

Left:, Quarry Hunslet EDWARD SHOLTO provides the power whilst SAMSON's rolling chassis obediently follows behind. These tests were very useful, resulting in some modifications to the brake gear, something that was better discovered at this stage rather than once the locomotive was finally assembled.

Below: A contrast in sizes – SAMSON's rolling chassis stands in front of 1889-built Marshall traction engine MARY MARGARET, the angle of the photograph rather misleading their relative sizes!

Right: The original photograph of SAMSON at Cornish Hush clearly reveals a negative clearance for the brake pull rods – something that has puzzled many an observer of that image. The increase in driving wheel size granted the new SAMSON some additional clearance, but the testing proved that this was insufficient, so the brake cross-shaft (the brake only acts on the right hand side of the locomotive and on the rear driving wheel only) was inverted with the pedestals that support it being mounted above the footplate rather than below. The assembly was then enclosed under a shaped panel.

Right: By Christmas 2015 the locomotive was nearing completion, with the boiler mounted onto the frames by expansion brackets (which secure it to the frames but allow for expansion when hot) at the rear and sturdy shaped plates at the front. David poses with the engine in its most advanced state then seen.

Left: The left hand side of SAMSON has the gears located there, which were enclosed within a riveted gear-guard. The engraving reveals the shape of this, which was copied for the new locomotive. The guard was test-fitted at this stage, requiring the bunker to be in position for final fitting.

Right: A close up of the driving, or coupled, wheels on the right hand (non-geared) side of the locomotive. The pipework for the pump has been fitted, there being a pipe into and out of the tank plus a delivery to the boiler. The water circulates through the pump all of the time the engine is working, water circulating unless diverted to the boiler when required.

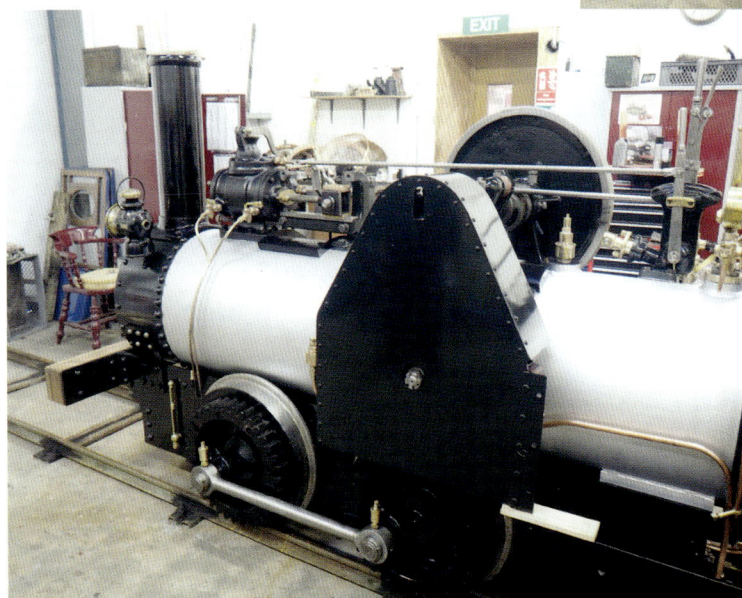

CHAPTER 8
CONSTRUCTION IN DETAIL
– THE ENGINE UNIT

PROBABLY THE ONE FEATURE on SAMSON that makes it stand out as 'different' to both the casual and educated observer is the presence of a flywheel alongside the boiler and the cylinder mounted atop. This will inevitably excite questions as to its pedigree – is it a traction engine on rails or a railway engine with a traction engine top. The actual term settled on over the years has been 'Traction Engine Locomotive' and this ably describes this engine too. The components that are mounted on top of and alongside the boiler are described as the 'engine unit' whilst the overall assemblage creates the 'locomotive' – again a useful distinction largely applicable to the Traction Engine Locomotive.

SAMSON has a single cylinder to provide its propulsion, the piston and connecting rod acting on a crankshaft from which the valve gear (and a water pump) is derived and which is fitted with a flywheel at one end and a pinion gear at the other. This is termed the 'first shaft' for purposes of describing this locomotive. The second shaft is actually a stub axle mounted low down on the left hand side crankshaft pedestal, which carries a large gear to span the gap between the pinion and the ring gear mounted onto the rear driving wheel. Through this 'drive train', mechanical gearing of 1:2·25 is attained, and so maximises the output of the cylinder. This chapter looks in detail at the construction of the new SAMSON's engine unit with a particular focus on the processes involved in creating working parts from scratch.

Right: Once the drawings had been completed by David, a start was made on the patterns needed for the castings. It had been decided early on in the project that parts would be built, so far as is possible or known, by the same methods as they would (or could) have been in 1874 when the original SAMSON was constructed. This ruled out extensive use of fabrications that might have been an option in 2013 and which could utilise modern metal cutting and welding techniques to produce pieces every bit as satisfactory mechanically, but perhaps a little lacking in the charm that castings exude when used to their best effect. This gathering of patterns included many of the cylinder components, including the valve chest, end covers and safety valve.

CYLINDER
FOR LOCOMOTIVE SAMSON

Drawn by D T Young

The process of pattern making is an art form. The pattern does not just resemble the shape of the desired component, it must allow for shrinkage of metal in the casting process; it must be mouldable in foundry sand and the pattern must be removable i.e. it cannot have shapes that would encapsulate the pattern such that it could not be withdrawn and finally allowance for machining should also be included. Where there are hollows or passageways to create, core boxes are used and the pattern must reflect the ability for the moulding to support a core (essentially the 'empty space' and supported by core 'prints' as part of the pattern) within it and to withstand the pouring of molten metal without moving.

Right: The flywheel rim is added to a disc of profiled plywood to create the embryonic pattern, made from machined blocks of mahogany (retrieved from old stair treads) cut at an angle so as to fit radially around the rim. This was mounted onto the faceplate of David's Schaublin Milling Machine, and rotated against the cutter (mounted on the horizontal spindle that this model is fitted with) to produce the uniform and circular outside profile of the flywheel.

Above: This pattern, for the cylinder block, shows the construction of a dense pattern with the basic shape being made up of laminations of blocks, then machined to the final profile. David's Smart & Brown lathe is employed on this work in this view.

Right: David with the completed flywheel pattern – the largest made for this project and so one where particular consideration had to be given to its manufacture (at the foundry) and shrinkage. The calculations for the flywheel itself were derived from engineering 'bible' 'A Manual of Machine Drawing and Design' by D. A. Lowe and A. W. Bevis, used extensively by David in his professional career and for his work at Beamish. This is an essential component of the design of SAMSON, offering proven solutions and calculations entirely appropriate to a project such as this one.

CRANKSHAFT AND SUPPORTS
FOR LOCOMOTIVE SAMSON

Drawn by D T Young

Right: Probably the most complex patterns produced for the project were for the two crankshaft pedestals, the pattern being modified in between castings to create a handed pair as the left hand casting would have to incorporate the mounting for the second shaft stub axle. Also seen here is the motion bracket pattern, the casting from which supports the two slidebars (also seen here) at their extremity from the cylinder block.

Below: The first purchase of castings was a healthy one and included cast iron and gunmetal to produce cylinder components and the crankshaft bearings. Also included are blanks – material cast for future transformation into nuts and bolts. Casting certificates were obtained for all materials used in order that a 'Technical Construction File' for the locomotive could be maintained, an essential part of introducing a new design steam locomotive into the public arena.

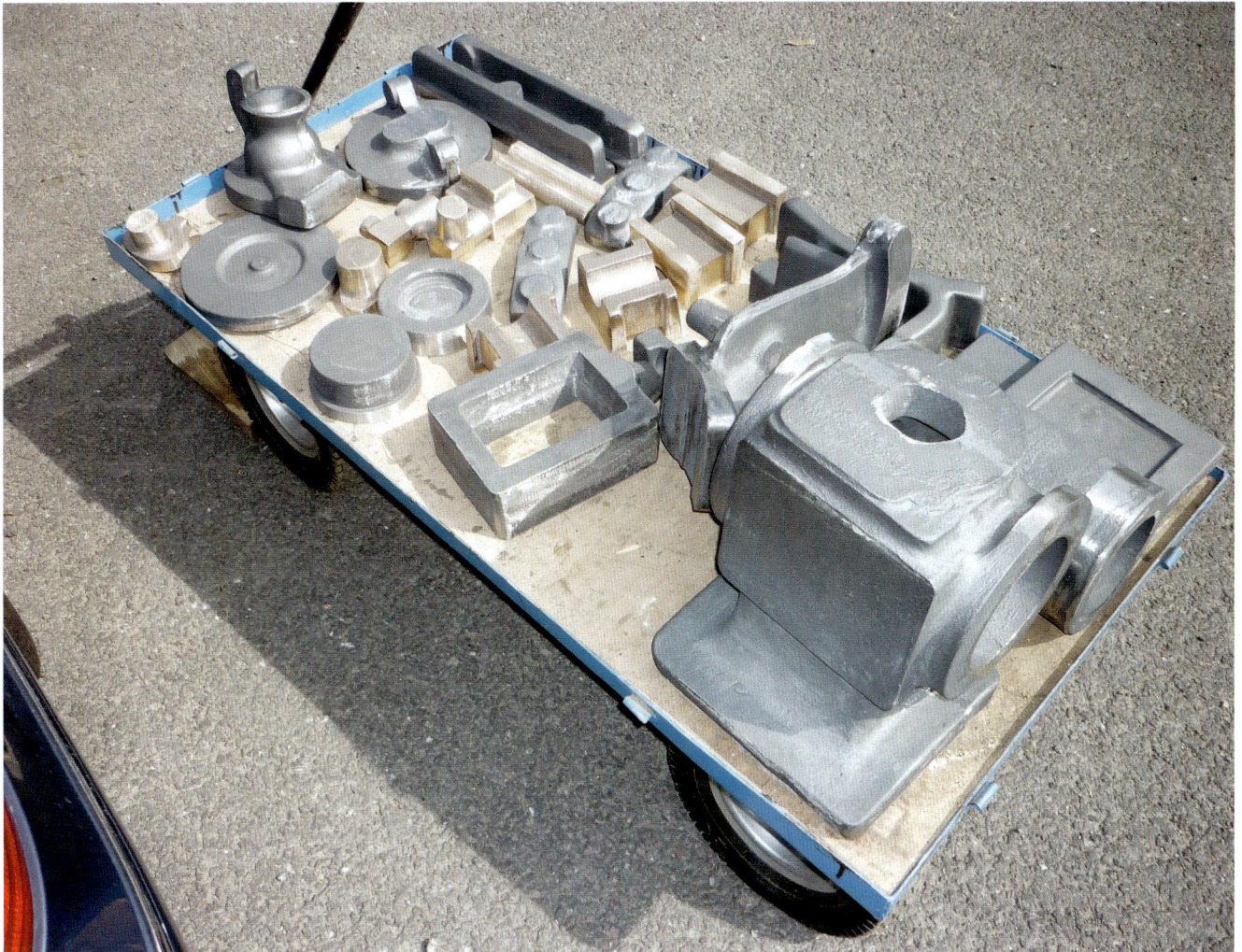

Left: The left hand crankshaft pedestal after casting. This was a formidable item, to make the pattern for, to cast (the moulder had several complex shapes to form and an undercut to incorporate) and to machine. The trouble is well worthwhile in creating a very satisfying piece of metal and one well capable of the job it must perform.

Below: The crankshaft was supplied as a profiled section at the same time as the frames, this substantial component requiring considerable machining work to transform it into the finished item. The first stage was to mill away as much excess material as possible before the blank was moved to the lathe.

Left: Set up in the Museum's Czechoslovakian made 'Tos' lathe, the advantage of removing the corners becomes clear as the shaft begins to take on its circular section. The 'striking' of the tool with intermittent cutting not only reduced the life of the tooling but work hardened the material being machined. In the past, such an item would have been forged, the hammering (by steam) both shaping and tempering the metal to give it the required strength as well as form.

Right: The crankshaft was machined to accept the connecting rod (big-end), eccentrics, eccentric for the water pump, flywheel, pinion and two journals which run in the bearings that support the assembly upon the pair of pedestals. Ingenuity was required to make sure that any dimensional variations on the surface were incorporated at this stage and that parts that had to be slid onto the shaft could clear the seats for other components before being settled tightly onto their own seating. The cranks on the shaft themselves were ground then dressed by hand to give them their very appealing curves.

Below: The crankshaft was installed into the pedestals after not a little etting up had been completed

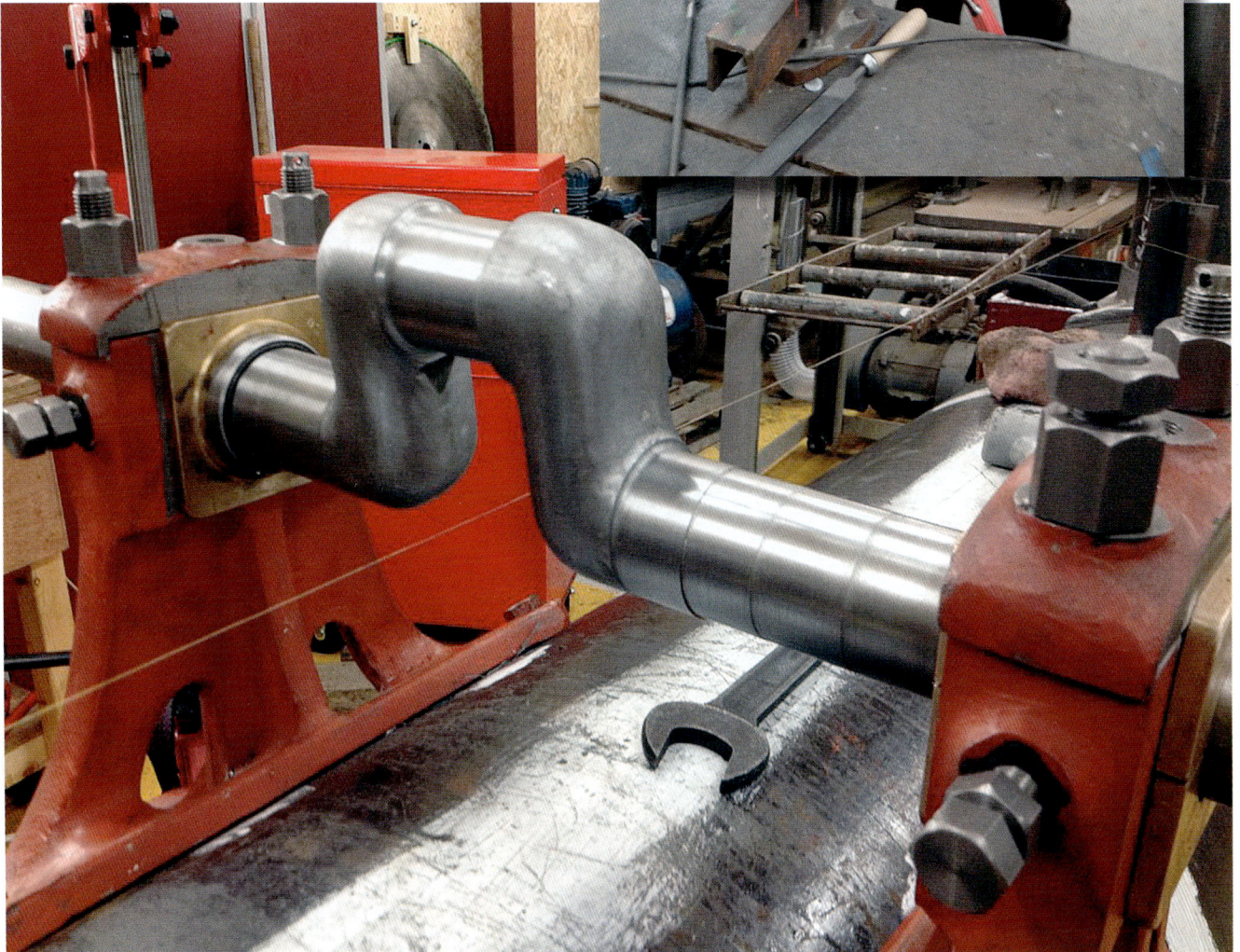

Right: A centreline was established on the boiler, there being no framework for the engine unit, piano wire being run from a temporary centre gauge behind the chimney to its partner at the rear of the barrel. David's mantra "never forsake your centreline" paid off and it was subsequently used not only for the mechanical components, but for establishing centres for the tubeplates and backhead.

Left: The positioning of the crankshaft pedestals was critical to the success of the whole engine and to ensure they sat square to each other on a circular form (the boiler barrel), these jigs were made to hold them securely and with a precise spacing between the cheeks which hold the bearings. Note the centreline wire passing through the centre of the jig. The pedestals could then be attached to the boiler by drilling and bolting (later into blind bushes – see Chapter 8).

Right: SAMSON is fitted with Stephenson valve gear, one of the most straightforward designs applied to steam traction and one which is reliable and relatively easy to set up. Two eccentrics are required to impart the forwards and backwards motion on the valve rod (which in turn directs steam into one end of the cylinder or the other), one for forward travel and one for travel in reverse. Additionally, an eccentric was required to drive the water pump. A cast eccentric is seen here, the off-centre hole being that through which the crankshaft passes. The 'eccentric' motion this will impart can clearly be seen here.

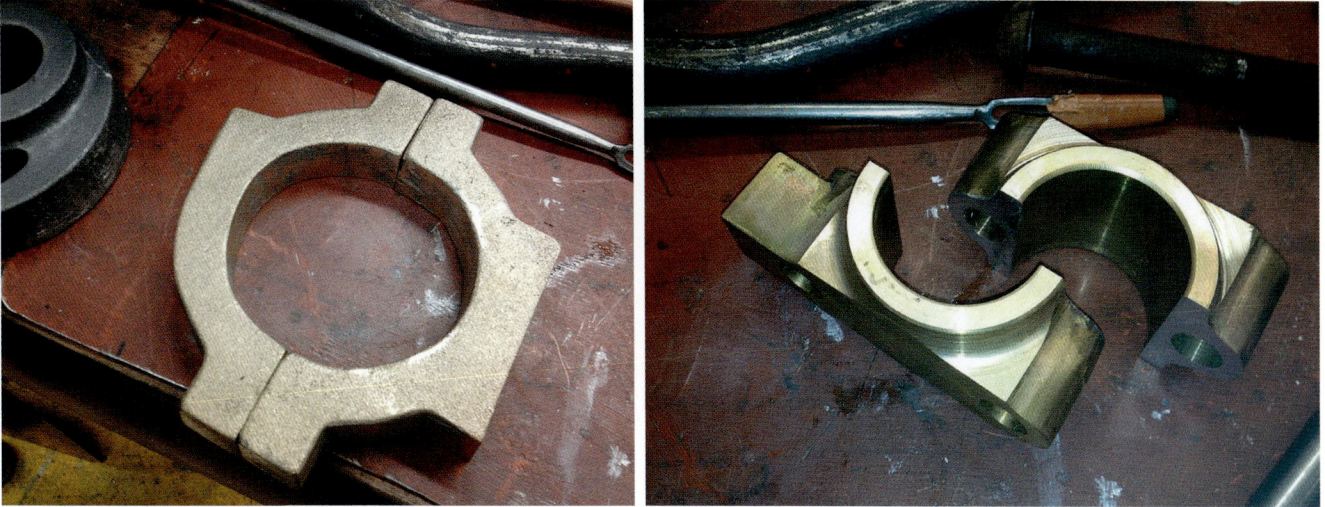

Above left: Around the eccentric is an eccentric strap, made of gunmetal (a type of bronze – an alloy of copper, tin and zinc which is resistant to water and steam and, with suitable lubrication, an ideal bearing surface for working parts) and formed in two pieces mated together for machining before they are bolted on the final assembly. These follow the travel of the eccentric and also include an oil reservoir and face onto which the eccentric rod itself is secured. Above right: The marine big end design is a simple way of attaching the connecting rod to the crankshaft, though does not allow for the adjustment offered by other arrangements. The bronze bearing is in two sections, which are joined by through-bolts which also accept the flared end of the connecting rod. An oil reservoir was also incorporated into this design, better suited to the 'violent' reciprocating motion of the big end and the narrow confines within which it must fit.

Below: The eccentrics are seen assembled together with their straps onto the crankshaft in this view, which also shows the marine type big end bearing in place.

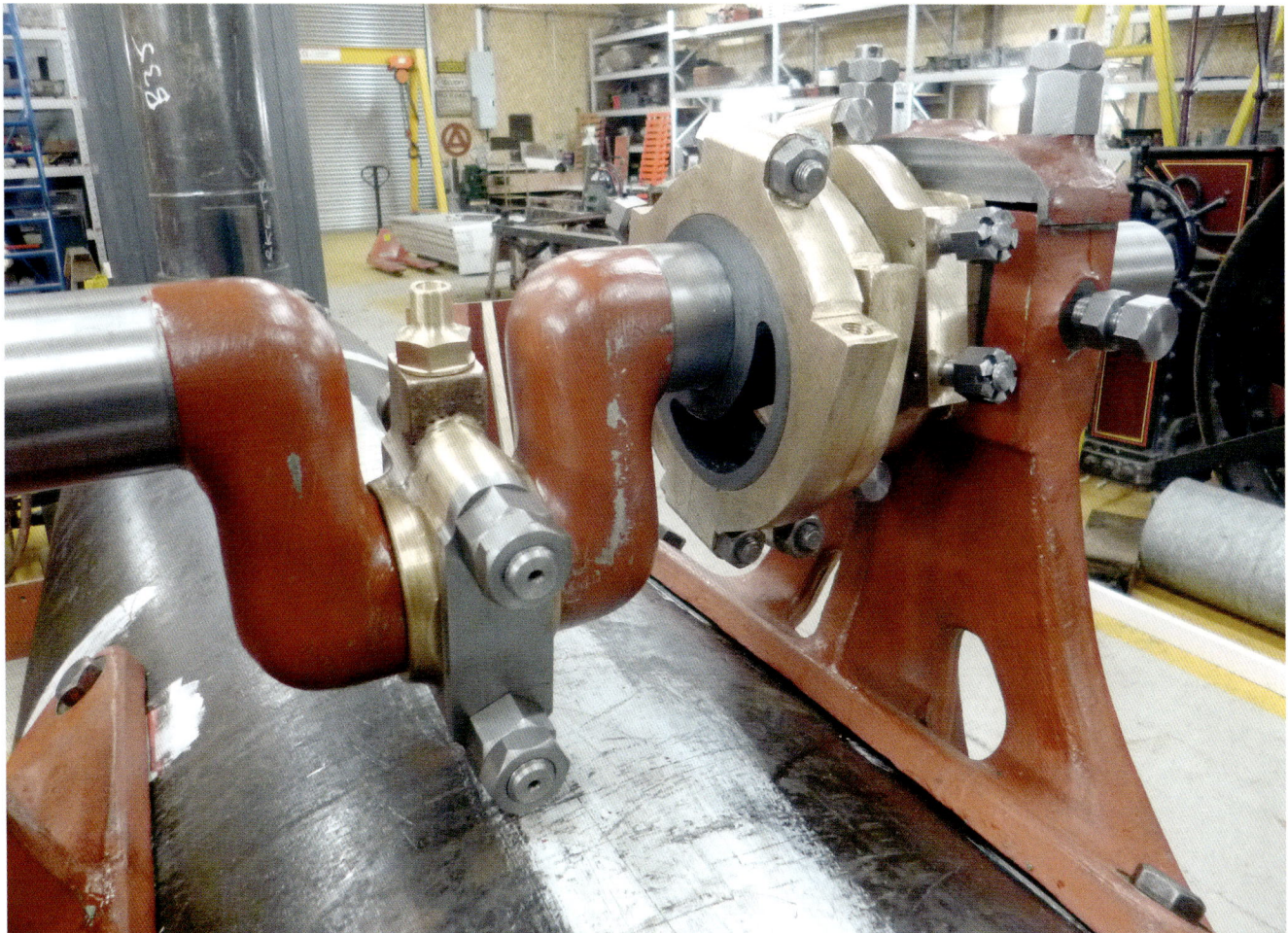

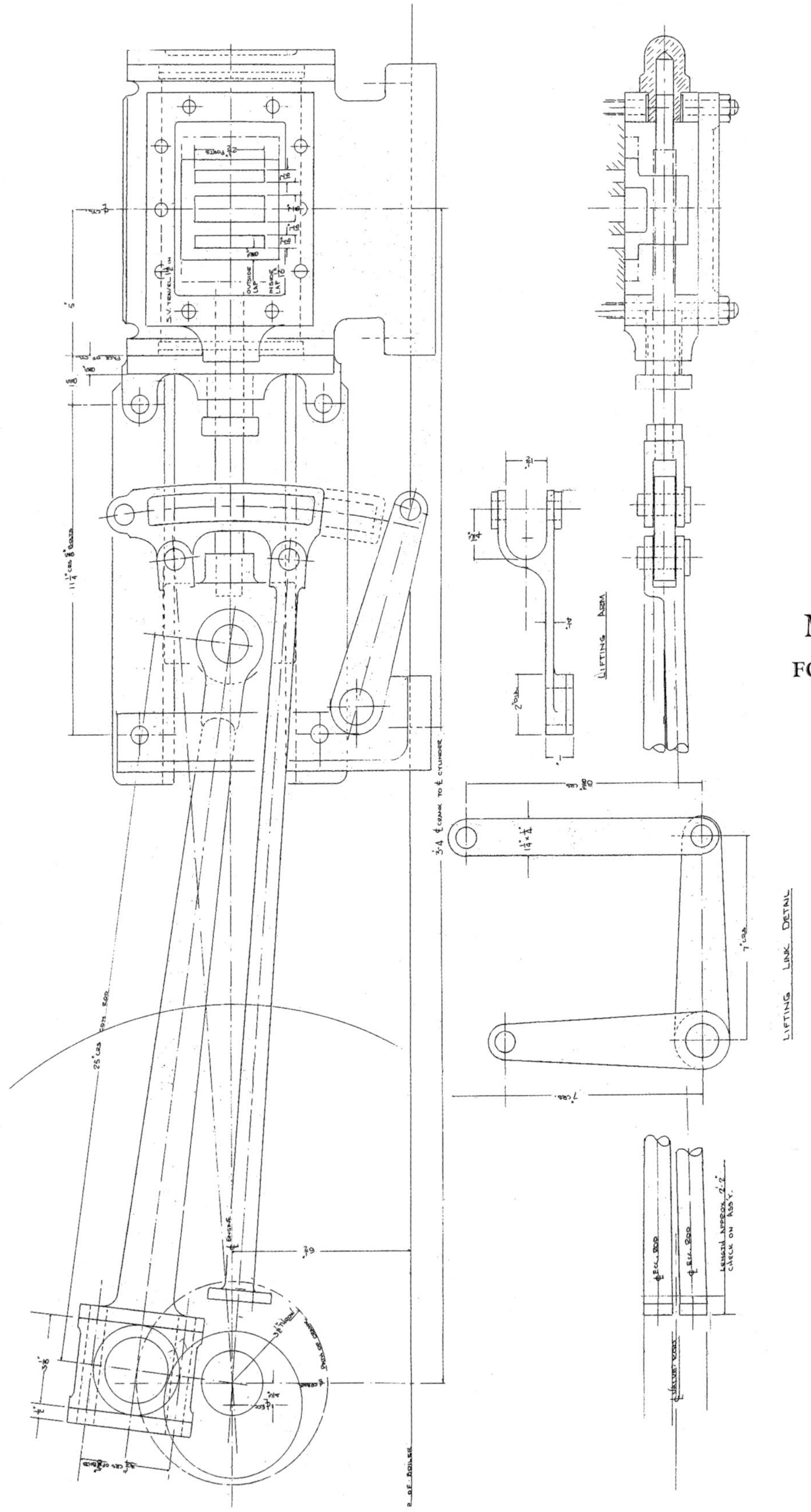

MOTION WORK
FOR LOCOMOTIVE
SAMSON

Drawn by D T Young

Above left: The reversing lever on a Traction Engine Locomotive is a very important component for the driver, not only acting as a means of changing direction, but also as a method to retard the locomotive's motion by moving the lever into the opposite direction of travel. SAMSON has only one brake block, which is only truly effective when the locomotive is already stationary, so the reversing lever is a vital component and one which offers a tactile satisfaction in the driver's grip – perhaps to inspire confidence more than anything else! Construction of the reversing lever began by profiling the handle/latch from a solid blank of steel, seen compared to the drawing prepared for this component. Above right: The completed reversing lever alongside the regulator handle (another item that should fall readily to hand), both of which are mounted onto the same cast stand, along with the water pump and associated valves.

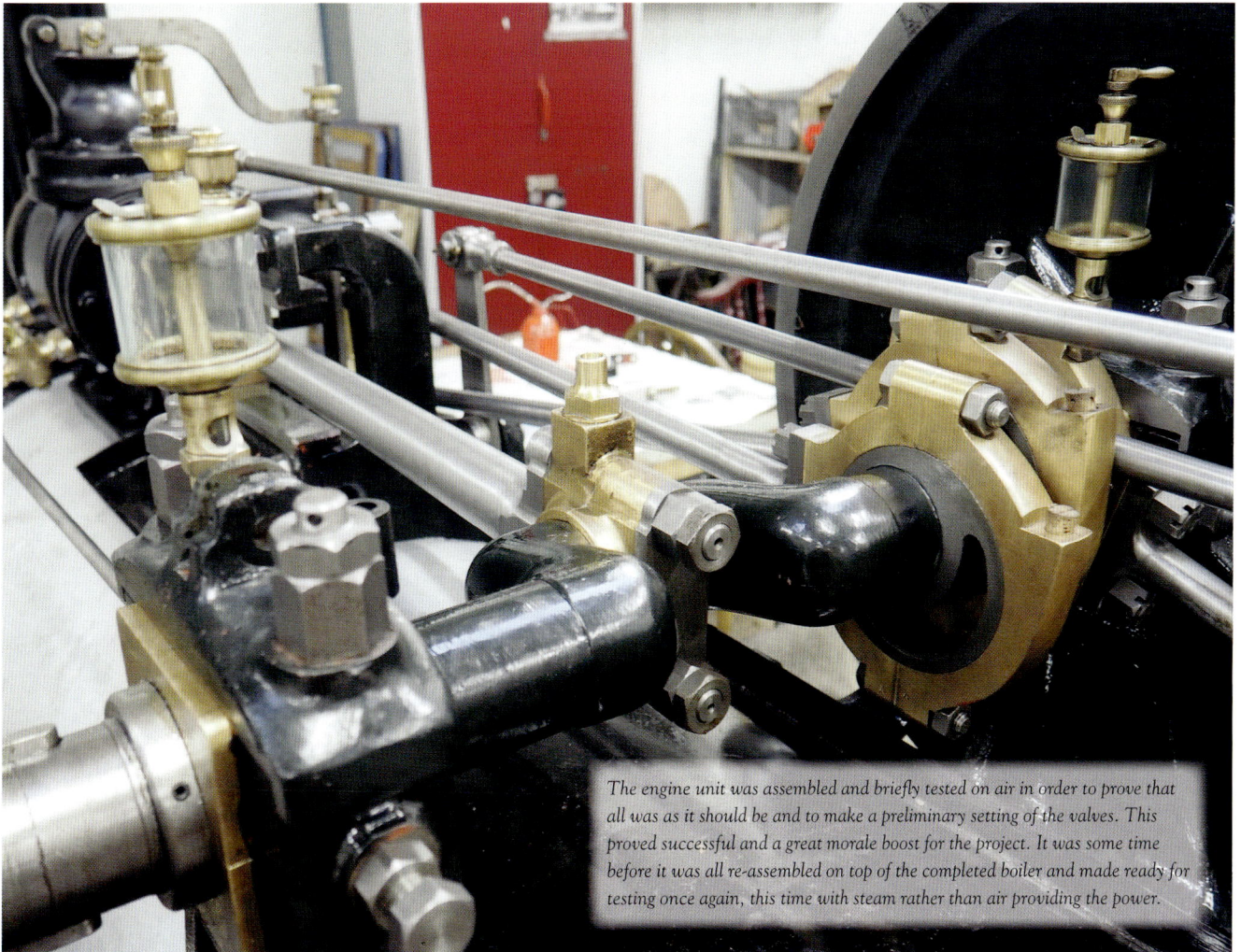

The engine unit was assembled and briefly tested on air in order to prove that all was as it should be and to make a preliminary setting of the valves. This proved successful and a great morale boost for the project. It was some time before it was all re-assembled on top of the completed boiler and made ready for testing once again, this time with steam rather than air providing the power.

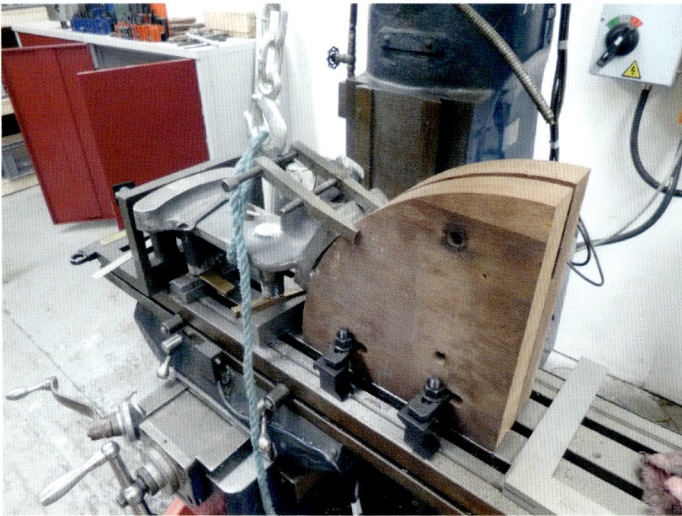

Above right: The valve gear on SAMSON *employs an inverted bell-crank for the lifting links, which move the expansion link, this being where the forward and backward eccentric rods meet and drive the valve rod, the lifting links altering the positon of the expansion link relative to the valve rod. The single expansion link was made from a piece of steel, chain drilled to create the internal aperture within which the die-block runs, as seen here prior to milling to final profile.*

Above left: One challenge in machining the large and heavy cast iron components was both handling them and securely mounting them onto the beds of machines. David made two very heavy duty mahogany brackets, shaped to the same profile as that of the boiler and to which the various castings could be bolted. This is the reverser pedestal including the pump mountings, set at 90 degrees on the wooden brackets on a Cincinnati milling machine at Beamish.

Below: To create the arc of the correct radius on the outside and inside faces of the expansion link, a device was devised and fitted to the milling machine table. With a threaded bar set at the desired angle, the arc was secure and could be fed through the statically positioned milling cutter, the arc being repeatable for each surface.

Left: Various jigs were used throughout construction. These three wooden discs enabled David to accurately calculate the Pitch Circle Diameter (PCD) for sizing the gears and ensuring that the teeth would engage in correct relation to one another.

Right: This is the centre spindle of the stub shaft for the intermediate (second shaft) gear. This shaft has to take a great deal of load, bearing the weight of the substantial gear and also engine load being transmitted to the ring gear on the driving wheel.

Right centre: In order to carry the intermediate gear, the second shaft, which is in reality a substantial bearing, was of generous proportions and also eccentric. This was to aid gear meshing and make precise adjustment possible and so the larger shaft was inserted into the pedestal casting, rotational through 360 degrees for adjustment, and then secured by the spindle which securely clamps the shaft into position.

Below: This view shows the shaft in position sans securing spindle. The eccentric nature of the bearing surface in relation to that section inserted into the casting can clearly be seen.

Above: The gears were machined locally by a specialist gear manufacturer from castings supplied by Beamish. The larger second shaft gear was quite an undertaking, including slender open spokes with a cross shape section through the spoke. The two gear rings for the driving wheels were a more straightforward proposition. Additionally the smaller pinion gear for the crankshaft was also machined by the same company, who made it such that it can be slid along its section of the crankshaft and so enable SAMSON to be taken out of gear. It is not known if the original locomotive had this feature, but later Stephen Lewin overtype locomotives, including Hops and Malt, did so and this enabled flexibility in their operation as they could act as static portable engines.

THE CYLINDER BLOCK

SAMSON's cylinder block would present a major challenge in patternmaking and so the principles established in W. J. Hughes' book 'Traction Engines Worth Modelling' were applied, by which the cylinder is built up in layers, the valve chest assembly being a separate component and itself built up in layers principally to enable easier access for machining the valve port faces. The issue of machining port faces was a very real one, after David spent a considerable amount of time using an adapted cordless drill to re-cut the port faces on No.18, whose valves had been re-machined but as a result no longer fitted the faces which they had spent a great many years wearing into a happy union with! The radius on the base of the cylinder block was machined by a contractor, as it was too large for the machinery available at Beamish. The block was then mounted onto the milling machine, as shown here, in order for various flat faces to be cut – in this case the two landings for the cylinder drain cocks.

Right: The cylinder block is next seen held captive on a Kearns Boring Machine, a potentially deadly piece of equipment but one vitally useful and which performs a number of functions in the hands of a skilled machinist. The Kearns Boring Machine was principally used to create a parallel and accurate bore through the casting. The casting process, in which a core print was used, had ensured that the cylinder block was hollow, but this was not sufficiently accurate for the cylinder to function. As a liner was to be fitted, a very high degree of accuracy to enable the liner to be pressed in to form an interference fit was also required.

Above left: Here the boring operation is in underway, with a boring bar running through the machine from headstock to tailstock. The cutting bar can be seen within the cylinder, the boring bar rotating whilst the bedplate to which the cylinder block is bolted travels along this length as the cut is made. Also visible here is the internal steam passageway – this conducts steam from the boiler (via the cylinder base) to the safety valve and regulator, and whence to the valve chest. The liner method avoided the need to create this passageway by complex coring and moulding at the casting stage, a method which was agreed upon early on in the project as a means of determining the overall feasibility of building the new SAMSON. Above right: The block has returned to the milling machine in order for the top surface to be faced in order to accept the safety valve, which forms an integral part of the cylinder and which is directly connected to the boiler via the passageway shown in the previous photograph.

Right: This is the underside of the safety valve casting, which also incorporates the regulator housing, seen to the right complete with the regulator itself in position. This slides against the machined face on the top of the main cylinder block casting where steam passes from the boiler, through the regulator and into the valve chest.

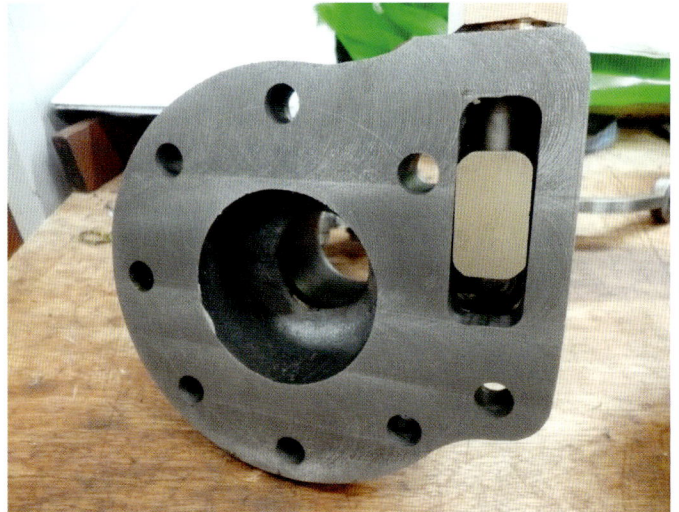

Below left: The valve chest face of the cylinder block has been machined and then drilled then tapped for the long studs to be inserted, onto which the layers of the valve chest are located.

Below right: The port face for the valve is seen on the left, machined complete with steam ports (the two outer slots) and the exhaust port (the larger central slot). To the right is the main valve chest itself, complete with valve rod, bushes and glands. The valve rod passes right through the chest, with the tail enclosed inside a tail-rod guide on the front of the chest.

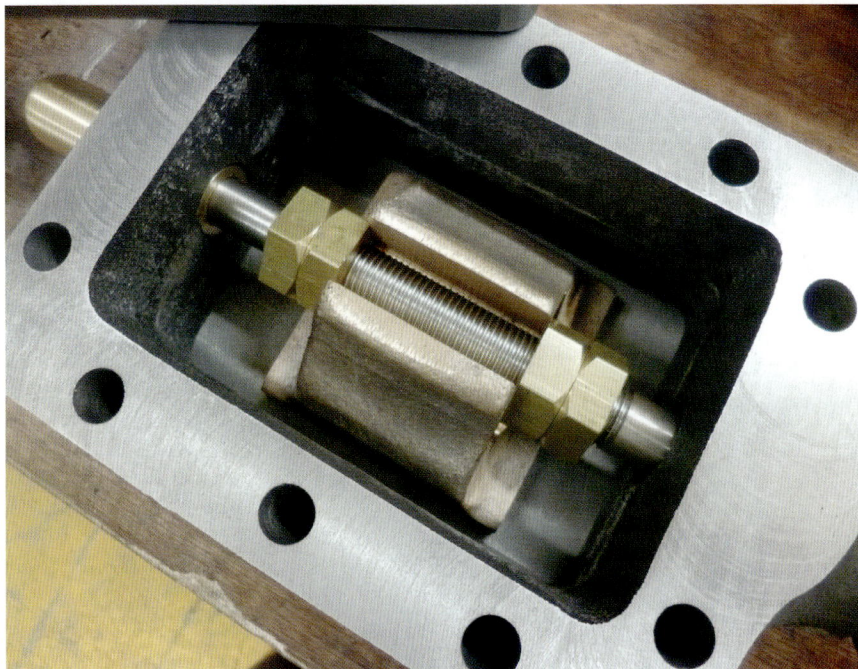

Left: The port face has been placed beneath the chest and the valve itself is now fitted onto the valve rod, its position being secured with locking nuts. The valve is able to float, steam pressure ensuring it sits against the port face, aided by two strips of sprung steel beneath the valve chest cover to ensure it does not pass steam from the live steam ports directly to the exhaust port.

Above left: The other side of the port face locates against the machined face of the cylinder block. This has had the live steam ports machined in this view, complete with the three passageways into each end of the cylinder through which steam is passed in order to work against the piston. The centre orifice is the route of the exhaust steam, which passes down into the block before turning through 90 degrees and exiting through the exhaust steam pipe which runs out of the front of the cylinder block and into the smokebox, turning again to point upwards and onto which a blastpipe nozzle is fitted. The action of the exhaust is significant in drawing the fire. Above right: The cylinder liner is clearly illustrated in this view, evident by the different colours of metal seen across the cylinder block end. The studs for the cylinder covers were still to be fitted at this point.

Centre right: The piston is assembled from a number of iron components with two bronze rings, which are slightly oversize but slit in order that they spring against the walls of the cylinder bore. This is then retained on a steel piston rod, to which it is bolted at one end. The other end of the rod is inserted into the crosshead and retained by a cotter.

Below left: The two gunmetal cylinder drain cocks were also made from scratch from David's own patterns, featuring plug cocks worked via a long rod from the footplate. The taper plugs were machined from straight bar, then bent to profile hot. Below right: The rear cylinder cover features two heavy spigots to which the two slidebars are attached. The alignment of these is critical, both to the cylinder (and its piston and piston rod) and the connecting rod to the crankshaft The articulation that enables this to be possible is achieved by the crosshead, which is attached to the piston rod and into which the connecting rod is located and rotates around a large pin held tightly in place within it. This slides backwards and forwards between the two slidebars, as is shown in the set up in this last photograph of this chapter. The engine unit has been covered here in some detail as it was felt it was likely to be of considerably interest to readers and also because it is illustrative of the huge amount of work and large number of precisely machined components that go into making up even a relatively simple steam engine.

CHAPTER 9
CONSTRUCTION IN DETAIL
– THE BOILER

The boiler barrel was purchased at the beginning of the project, as it would play a fundamental structural role when constructing the engine unit. The specification required a drawn-tube, meaning there is no seam along the barrel. This reduces the need to inspect and test a welded seam and will ease future maintenance and inspections. The barrel itself was made in Italy, supplied by a German company via an agent in Lancashire. The white paint here marks the longitudinal lines every quarter-section, essential to alignment and placement of the many attachments this barrel would receive and applied with the barrel standing vertically and guided by a plumb line.

A S HAS BEEN DISCUSSED EARLIER, the exact nature of the original SAMSON's boiler is not certain, though the non-depending or 'marine' firebox seems most likely. During the research phase it became apparent that the boilers employed on the Heywood locomotives described in Chapter 3 were of potentially very similar design and dimensions to that which would be most suitable for the new SAMSON. With KATIE's boiler available for inspection, and a set of drawings very kindly supplied by James Waterfield, engineer and boiler designer Graham Morris was able to produce a set of drawings for SAMSON's new boiler. These were then submitted to a notified body, in this case Royal Sun Alliance (RSA – now British Engineering Services) for scrutiny and formal approval.

The pressure system also includes devices to monitor water level, add more water (via the pump and injector) and safety valves.

SAMSON has been fitted with an injector, where none was previously fitted, as a precaution against the failure of the pump or an inability

Left & right upper: Within months of delivery, the barrel had been placed into the frames and had the chimney fitted (a morale booster!). The first crankshaft pedestal has been offered up to the barrel in these views, the project still being very raw bare metal at this stage.

Left: A view into the chimney, another drawn tube and with the distinctive Stephen Lewin chimney rim riveted in place (by David and his wife Maureen!). Chimneys and smokebox doors give so much character and therefore identity to a steam locomotive and so this was particularly important to get right.

Right: Another haul of castings from the foundry included these gunmetal components for the main steam manifold and two flanges for the clack valve assembly.

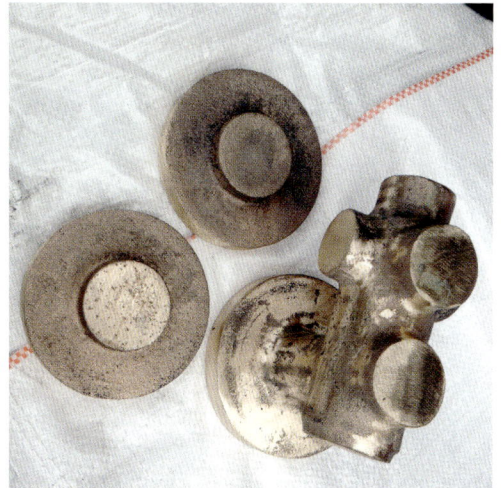

for the engine unit to be turned over. This is a Penberthy injector of standard commercial design. The locomotive is also fitted with an additional safety valve, to supplement the Salter Spring Balance type mounted on the cylinder block. This gives an assurance that the boiler can evacuate steam even where this is being raised at the boiler's maximum steaming rate. The rear three quarter view engraving suggests only one gauge glass was fitted on the boiler backhead above the firebox door, with test or try cocks giving a back-up measure of water level inside the boiler. As the Heywood design of boiler demonstrated that a pair of gauge glass fittings would fit, and because it was felt two glasses would be more appropriate than the original's arrangements, then a pair of gauge glasses were incorporated into the new SAMSON's design.

Arrangements were made with the Severn Valley Railway (SVR) for their Bridgnorth boiler works to assemble the boiler, and so they

would also apply for the CE (Conformité Européene – European Conformity) mark that would be required under the Pressure Equipment Directive (PED). Graham Morris' drawings carefully specified all of the materials to be used in the boiler's construction, covered by the Pressure System Safety Regulations (PSSR) and utilising approved suppliers with a traceable document trail behind every component.

RSA surveyors would also inspect the boiler at key stages during its construction and oversee the cold, hydraulic and steam tests before issuing the appropriate certification, at which point the SVR would affix a plate to the boiler shell to confirm its conformity and display critical information regarding its design and test pressures, year of manufacture etc.

FEED PUMP & REVERSER
FOR LOCOMOTIVE SAMSON

Drawn by D T Young

Above left: The steam manifold has multiple roles, including the mounting for the whistle (a Burrell design to give SAMSON a distinct note compared to other steam locomotives at Beamish), pressure gauge, injector steam valve and a filling plug for the boiler when empty (something all boilers really should have but so often don't, for convenience). The sprung whistle valve is arranged such that a short 'pop' is possible, or a long and shrill 'blast', as the occasion demands.

Above right: SAMSON is (as the original was) fitted with a positive displacement pump driven from the crankshaft This draws water from the tank and circulates it either to the boiler via the clack valve or back to the tank, depending on the position of the valve and the need for boiler feed at any given time. Such pumps are extensively employed on traction engines and steam rollers and can be set such that the volume of water added matches the rate of evaporation within the boiler. The raw casting is seen 'chucked' in the lathe (and rotating) with a boring bar inserted into the chamber to machine the bore for one of the valves.

Right: The finished assembly, something of a work of art, mounted onto the reversing lever quadrant (which also supports the pump rod chamber itself as well as the reversing lever and regulator handle). The small handle visible is a priming cock to assist in the initial lifting of water from the tank, the larger handle is the by-pass valve which controls the rate of flow through the circuit, to the boiler or returning to the tank.

Above left: The smokebox door is of the flat-plate type, lodged in place by two clips and tightened by a rotating clamp of distinctively Lewin design. The plate for the smokebox door ring is being cut here. Above right: With the centre removed, the outer profile is cut, using a plasma cutter and adapted trammel to give the correct radius.

Left: With a flat strip rolled to the same circumference as the radius of the front plate, the two have been welded together and dressed to the finished profile. This work was carried out by Chris Armstrong, who became increasingly involved with the project at this stage.

Right: David made the door handle to replicate those seen on other Stephen Lewin locomotives – to the connoisseur the maker and origin of a steam locomotive can be identified by this handle alone!

Above: The smokebox tubeplate was fitted into the barrel and then the drilling commenced again Note David's tool tray mounted on the clamp holding the barrel to the bed of the drill! Repeated changing of drill collets and bits is required to pilot then drill out each hole, so such a tray is a prudent tool to prevent items becoming lost.

Below: The angle ring that mates the backhead to the boiler barrel is a substantial piece of steel, turned from a solid ring by Dyer Engineering, a local firm often carrying out specialised work for the Museum. Chris and David persuade the ring onto the end of the boiler barrel using heat both inside and outside the barrel to make it more 'receptive' to the process.

Left: Here the ring has been fitted onto the barrel (using no small amount of heat to assist) and prepared for drilling. The backhead has already been drilled (clamped to the ring to ensure alignment of the holes).

Right: The boiler was set up on rollers beneath the radial arm drill in the machine shop. With a centre hole drilled, a full bore hole was then made. With 44 holes in total, this process was time consuming and heavy work for David, assisted by Chris, the boiler barrel being rotated by hand and with some precision in its positioning being required.

Left: The smokebox tubeplate (left) and flanged firebox (complete with tubeplate already welded to the barrel) were supplied by Israel Newton & Sons, a boilermaker with a 200 year tradition and eminently able to provide flanged components for boilers of traditional design. Such shapes could have been fabricated and welded, but it was felt that Samson should resemble as far as possible the original, which would entail hot flanged plates like this despite their greater cost. It also avoids square corners, a radius on a plate enabling it to 'breathe' when expanding and contracting (though in the long term cracking can be result).

Right: So far the boiler preparation had been carried out at Beamish, but the assembly was to be carried out at Bridgnorth on the SVR, so the components were moved to the boiler works there and Chris, Matt Ellis and the author spent a total of five days assisting with the final construction work. Here the pre-drilled holes are reamed using an air powered motor. This gives a slightly oversize hole, needed for the hot rivets, and also ensures the hole aligns perfectly with no step between plates from which cracks in rivets could propagate.

Left: Once again the portable hearth is seen in action as ¾ inch rivets are heated in readiness for insertion into the reamed holes.

Left:With the rivet inserted and the air jamming tool placed up against it, the outer head is hammered and shaped. The jammer also has a repeating action, additionally hammering the rivet home. The holes had all previously had their edges removed (by creating a small chamfer), again a precaution against sharp edges that could lead to cracking and rivet failure.

Above left: The dramatic process of hammering a hot rivet into place and forming the distinctive domed head. Above right: Attaching the backhead to the firebox barrel proved to be challenging to set up, requiring the jammer to work off the floor vertically whilst the assembly was bolted to a machine bed placed in the middle of the works. Some of the rivets fitted also needed to be ground flush, as that piece of plate would have to fit snugly against the angle ring flange at the bottom of the boiler.

Right: A close up of the countersunk rivets after the heads have been ground flush. Deeper countersinks were required, along with shorter rivets, to form the shallow head and ensure sufficient grip for the rivet and minimal material to be removed using an angle grinder.

Left: The front tubeplate is seen after riveting into the barrel. Each rivet is inserted in what seems an endlessly repeated process whereby adjacent holes are tightly bolted to clamp them and ensure the rivet closure has the maximum purchase. The bolts were as tight as could physically be managed, yet after the rivet next to a bolt was inserted, hammered and had cooled, such was its purchase that the adjacent bolt was now slack and could often be removed by fingertip.

Right: Attaching the backhead involved a set sequence of work to ensure that it could actually be riveted. First the angle ring was attached to the barrel, and then the backhead was attached to the firebox barrel. This assembly was then inserted into the main boiler barrel and the backhead riveted to the angle ring, all the while having to ensure that everything remained in its correct position. Two stays of Monel Steel (favoured on the BR Standard steam locomotives) were then fitted, to support the front of the firebox (so this non-depending design is actually 'slightly' depending) and so not have to rely entirely on the tubes themselves to do this.

Left: With the boiler shell complete the tubes could then be inserted. The front tubeplate holes were fractionally larger than the firebox tubeplate, to aid insertion of the tubes. These are then expanded into the tubeplates using an air motor at one end to drive a tube expander, its tapered rollers driving it into the tube and rolling the tube outwards to create a tight fit. At the other end, seen here and in this case inside the firebox, a second expander is held on an extension bar, any tendency of the tube to twist as it is expanded at the other end actually working against this expander to tighten it at this end and so quickly 'brake' any rotation that might occur. Once one end has been expanded, the other end can be expanded without the additional tools being required.

Inset: A close up of the tube expander, consisting of a set of tapered rollers which are inserted into the tube end. Through this the tapered mandrel is inserted, this being driven by an air motor (or ratchet if done by hand), the action of this being to rotate the rollers as the mandrel forces them outwards against its taper.

Right: To secure the cylinder block to the boiler barrel, these 'carrot' bolts (the reason for their name being apparent from their shape) are used, inserted narrow end upwards through the barrel and into the block. The nuts are fitted on top, the tightening action of these drawing the taper of the bolt tight into the barrel and forming a steam-tight joint. The holes were to allow capture of any bolts that might initially rotate or be dropped during their fitting – a precaution that ensured they were all safely fitted without mishap!

Left: A view into the boiler from the hand-door located at the top of the smokebox tubeplate. The tubes are readily apparent, as they disappear away from the camera towards the firebox. The circular stubs visible all around the barrel are the blind bushes welded into position and into which the various external structural fittings, such as the crankshaft pedestals, are bolted. This method ensures the barrel is guaranteed to be steam-tight and makes it far easier to fit bolts without having to locate nuts, by hand, within the boiler itself.

Right: The impressive casting for the firebox door surround and door is shown here. This also acts as a support for the rear of the firebars and a means of attaching a damper. It carries David's name as the principal builder of Samson, cast in iron for all time.

Left: The completed firebox with firebars (eight in number) in place and firebricks trimmed to fit within the bridge, which also supports the front of the firebars. It will never be seen this clean again!

Below: SAMSON's first test begins. A lengthy period of warming the boiler through was followed by a series of steam tests to make adjustments and ensure the boiler and its safety features were performing correctly. It was then steamed for the boiler inspector, and upon receiving his favourable verdict, work to fit the lagging and cladding could be begin…

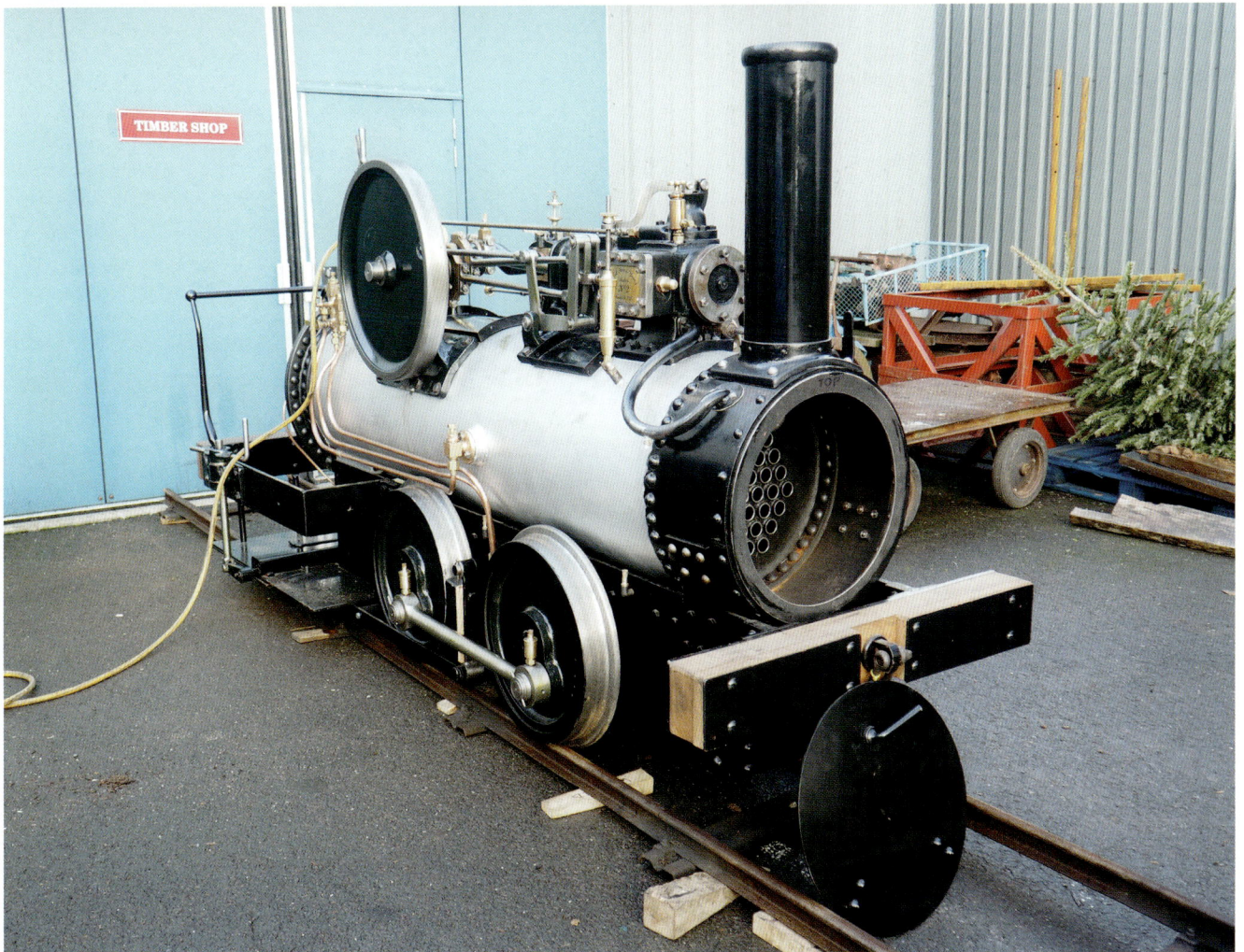

CHAPTER 10
SAMSON'S DEBUT

Above: The last views of the pristine firebox, seen from above and below the firebars. Approximately a quarter of the way back from the tubeplate is the bridge, which carries the two firebricks which prevent the small combustion chamber being clogged with coal and ash. Beneath this bridge is a removable plate which performs the same function from below. The fusible plug is visible screwed into the underside of the firebox crown, this being a lead-filled safety device designed to melt if uncovered by absence of water above the crown and act to extinguish the fire with steam and alert the driver and fireman to the problem and in doing so protect the boiler from potentially catastrophic damage. This is very much a safety device of last resort and its failure would have to be reported to HMRI – Her Majesty's Railway Inspectorate.

O N THE 12 JANUARY 2016 the first fire was lit inside SAMSON's slender firebox. Allowing a day for the engine to thoroughly warm through, the following day the fire was re-lit and steam pressure was raised to 55 psi, approximately half the working pressure. This enabled the engine unit to be test run and a session of fault finding to be undertaken. To the delight of all, the engine ran very well and whilst minor teething problems manifest themselves, SAMSON, and David's engineering skills, were able to give a very good account of themselves and so spur the project on to completion.

Left: The first test occurred when filling the boiler with water. The fusible plug was removed and the boiler filled until water poured through the hole. This was compared to the level evident (or not) in the gauge glasses, confirming that the water level would have to be out of sight in the gauge glass (a very serious error) in order to create a 'dropped plug'. Had the water been evident in the glass, whilst flowing through this hole, then it would indicate a misalignment of the gauge glass cocks. As this was a new boiler such a problem was very unlikely, but this check verified the execution of the design to be correct.

Above left: The very first fire is lit – newspaper and kindling being used to give a very gentle warmth, the boiler and all of the fittings attached to it never having been hot together before. Above right: The fire developing and spreading across the firebars. The damper door below is open to allow air to pass up through the firebars and excite the fire. Usually the damper door would be closed when the firehole door is open and there is no steam to operate the blower (and draw the fire forwards towards the tubeplate), but for photographic purposes a more exciting image of flames leaping out of the door was preferred!

Below: The pristine chimney is no more as the first wreaths of smoke drift upwards.

Right: Dusk begins to wrap SAMSON at the end of its first day as a 'working' locomotive, the warming fire burning through and the temporary Edwardian motor car lamp sat in place to add to the atmosphere.

Inset: Day two and another fire has been lit within the already very warm boiler of SAMSON. After a few hours the very first signs of life become visible as the pressure gauge needle, suitably labelled, lifts off its stop and reveals SAMSON as a living machine for the very first time.

As pressure climbed over 30psi the drain cocks were opened and the cylinder warmed through before the reverser was set forwards and for the first time on steam, SAMSON's chimney gave its first deep chuff and the scene became obscured by steam.

David at the controls of the locomotive he had spent three years dreaming about and three years building.

Right: After some gentle running of the engine and testing of the water pump, the smokebox door was removed to enable inspection of the tubeplate, which was very pleasingly dry with no leaks or dribbles and only one rivet offering anything to cause interest, and even that was nothing to worry about. This was a real credit to the boilersmiths at Bridgnorth who had created such a tight vessel. Above the tube nest is a door, removable to enable boiler washouts to be carried out and to enable the carrot bolts which secure the cylinder block to the boiler barrel to be fitted.

At the bottom of the tubeplate is a washout plug, again used during a boiler washout and through which the detritus and water flow. A similar plug is fitted at the top of the backhead, to enable the lance through which pressurised water is pumped to be directed across the top of the firebox and down the sides. Keeping the internal surfaces of the boiler clean is vital to its long-term structural integrity and also its efficiency.

Additives are also placed into the water supply (directly into the water tank) to inhibit corrosion in three ways: oxygen scavenging, tannin to neutralise acidity and a chemical to keep dissolved solids in suspension so that they can be exhausted via the blow-down valve at the base of the boiler.

Above left & right: Samson is fitted with four sets of identifying marks. The first is its name, painted onto the boiler cladding directly rather than cast on a plate. This was judged to be more in keeping with its origins and also reflected on what was the original's probable nick-name rather than its formal identification. The second is a plate on the smokebox which carries the legal details required for the boiler as a pressure vessel under the Pressure Equipment Directive (PED) and which acts as the CE mark for the applicable standards (in this case, the Pressure System Safety Regulations). This is affixed by the manufacture, in this case the Severn Valley Railway.

The valve chest carries an engraved brass plate stating the engine's number (No.2 in the Beamish register, No.1 is the STEAM MULE) and year of construction (2015). It also carries the name 'David Thomas Young' as its maker, lettering repeated in cast iron on the firebox door surround, leaving no doubt as to who played such an essential part in the recreation of one of the lesser known but undeniably characterful steam locomotives.

Left: On the boiler top, tucked between the crankshaft and steam turret (see page opposite), is another safety valve, a requiremnt of modern boiler regulations.

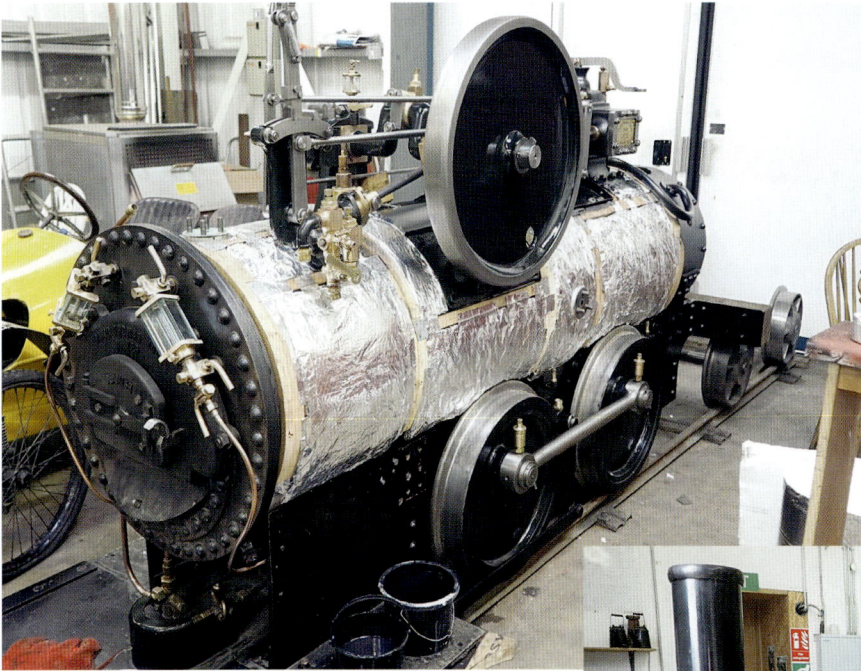

Left: With steam testing completed and the satisfactory conclusion of the statutory process whereby the boiler was witnessed in steam by the Museum's boiler inspector (including safety valve/accumulation tests), the process of cladding the boiler began. This was a job that David was quite happy to admit was not one he would care to repeat! A framework of wooden crinolines was made, to support the complex shapes of the cladding pieces. The spaces between these were then filled with a modern and thermally-efficient foil-backed insulation, panels being made up to fit within the wooden frame. Additional foil and tape was used to seal these and create a snug fit.

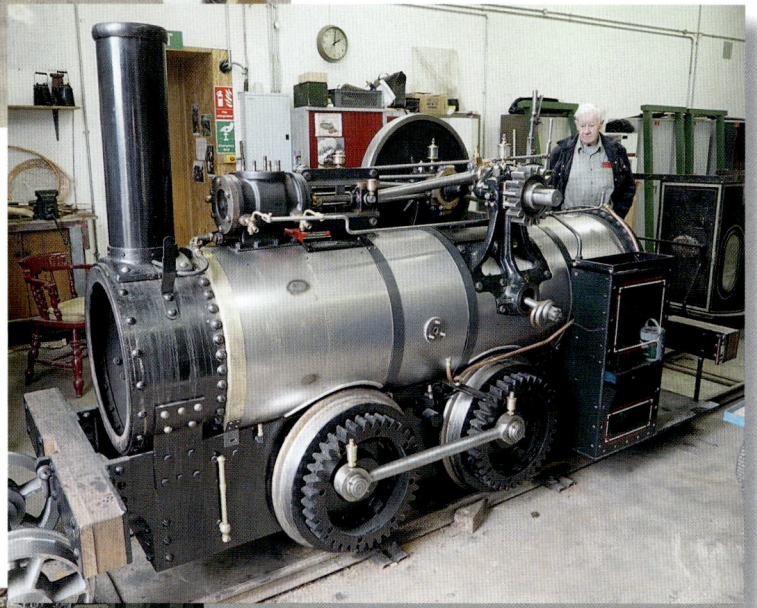

Right: The cladding sheets were always going to offer David something of a challenge, and this proved to be the case. With so many fittings and brackets to fit around, as well as the frame position and proximity of the driving wheels to consider, the panels were each made to individually fit, working from the rear of the locomotive forwards.

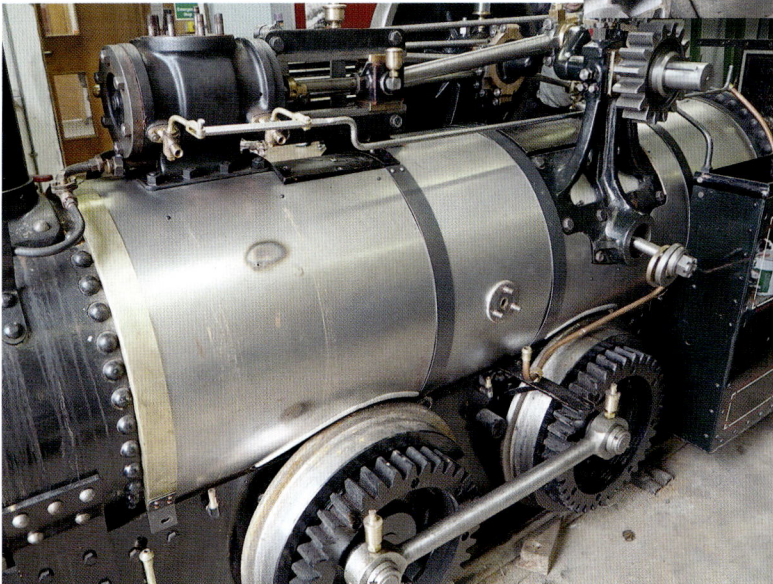

Left: Boiler bands were also made at the same time, the front being in brass and formed of four sections in order to include the front piece which encloses the lagging from that angle and gives the final, neat, appearance in this area. Whilst brass, it would be painted to match the others. Also visible here are the half-round beading strips fitted around the cut-outs to accommodate the driving wheels. Cleary visible too is the intricate shaping required to fit around the pedestals and other brackets, clack valve pads and oil trays. It was then time to start the final painting...

PAINTING...

Almost as soon as the bunkers had been manufactured there was an urge to paint and line them in order to give an impression of what the finished locomotive was going to look like. The colour chosen was Dark Green (from the Craftmaster Paints range and which almost looks black in some conditions), which is suitably ambiguous in varying light as the black and white photograph would suggest about the original Samson.

The first step was to paint the bunkers, the process involving several layers built up through two primers, up to four undercoats (a highly pigmented black) and four topcoats. Each was flatted down in between coats, the last also being flatted before the lining was applied.

Above: The master panel produced for the livery sample (see page xiv) was referred to throughout, and the straight lines marked then masked with tape. The indented corners were marked using a compass, then painted free-hand.
Right: With the first application complete (a deep maroon shade), the tape is removed to reveal this layer of lining. It was then allowed to fully harden before the masking for the next application was applied.

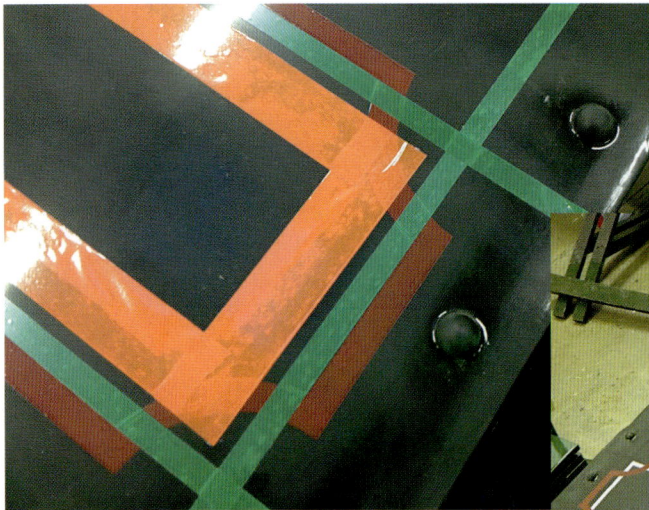

Above: The white lining was set behind the maroon, and some careful masking was required in order to ensure it 'laced' in the correct manner at each corner – easier said than done!

Right: With all of the tape removed the bunkers now begin to reveal the lining style to its full. It did not slavishly copy what was apparent on the original locomotive, rather used a number of styles that appear to have been applied to Lewin's locomotives, with a bit of creative flair to suit the new locomotive.

Above: Gently cutting back any paint from where it wasn't required, followed by flatting with a green pan scourer more or less rendered any such imperfections invisible. Once fully cleaned then tack-clothed to remove dust, the bunkers received two coats of varnish. All of the paints used were from the Craftmaster range (including the varnish), whilst the lining paint was a US product known as 'One Shot' – its superb coverage meaning lining tape can swiftly be removed once the paint is applied in a single coat.

Above: Care was taken to ensure that any rough areas or points where paint had crept underneath the tape were tidied up before varnishing. This was accomplished using a blade, working systematically around each panel as the author demonstrates here.

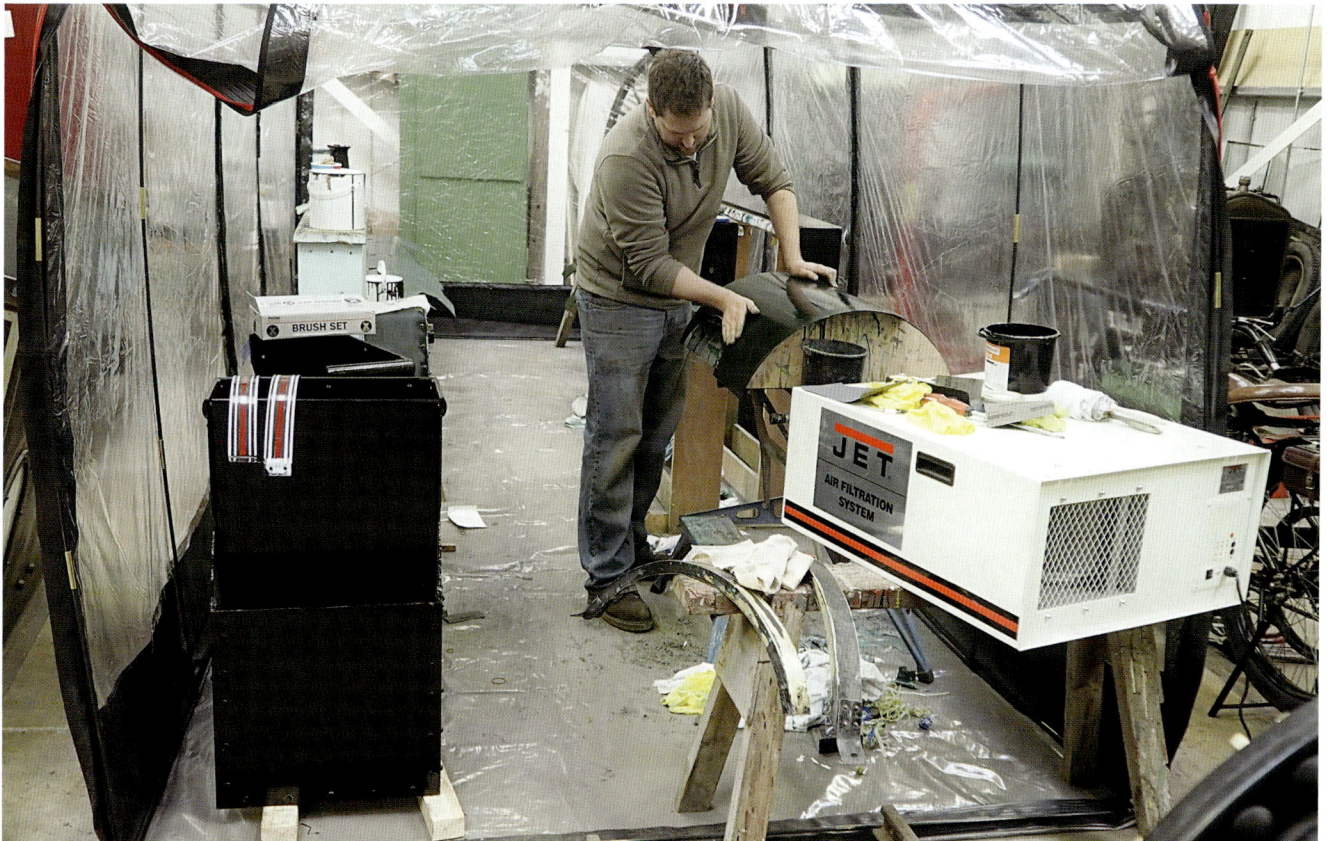

Above: The cladding presented its own challenges, not least due to its awkward shape to paint. A car storage tent was set up to create a dust-free atmosphere and each cladding sheet was systematically treated, building up layers of primer, undercoat, topcoat and varnish. Whilst this paint shop was rather Heath Robinson, it was effective.

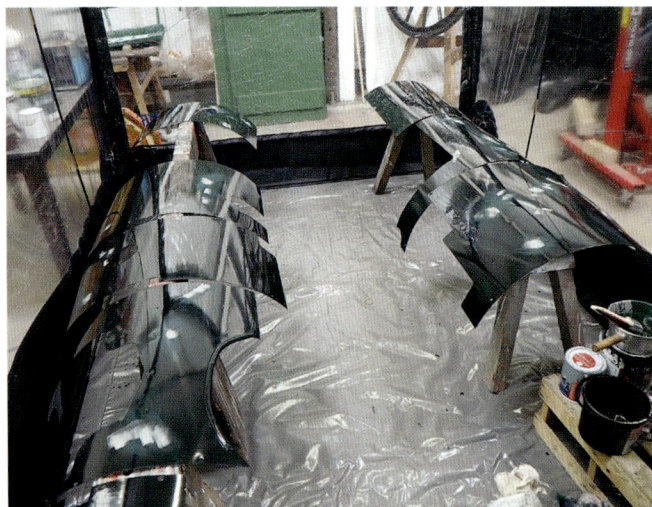

Above: The cladding sheets are seen laid out on trestles to dry. A dust extractor was used throughout the process to remove as much airborne contamination as possible. As can be seen, the advantage of the car storage tent is that the floor is sealed to the sides, reducing the hardest to manage form of dust contamination, that from the ground.

Right: To assist with the painting and preparation of the cladding sheets, a form of jig was made onto which they could be sat, then flatted and painted. This prevented flexing and enabled long brush strokes to be used along their full length, without deforming or contacting another surface at the beginning or end of the brush stroke. The author spent a great deal of time in this tent in the closing stages of the project!

The final adornment for SAMSON was the fitting of a suitable lamp. A railway lamp would have been unsuitable for a locomotive that would have had very little contact with the wider World, so a copper Georgian lamp was obtained via the online auction site that has so transformed access to such items. The lamp was an assemblage of parts and David rebuilt it into a more durable form.

The lamp also lacked any means of mounting it (having been a hand-held lamp, despite its size and weight), this being addressed by the removal of one glass pane and substitution with a sheet of copper to which a bracket was mounted. The bracket itself was copied from a Miller oil lamp in the author's collection and so is of more or less correct provenance. A burner was sourced and the lamp trialled (to ensure the silver soldered joints did not become loose).

A photograph taken on the evening of the day the boiler cladding was carefully fitted (wrapped in cellophane to protect it!), the bands added, name applied and other details completed. It was the first glimpse of Samson in its complete form and the first sight of this side of the locomotive since 1904 or earlier. The artificial lighting does not flatter this view, but it is included as it was a significant one for the project and those involved with it.

REFLECTING UPON THE PROJECT

Beamish's SAMSON has been built to endure. How long it will remain operational for will be a decision for those that follow in the future, but it will doubtless witness the passing of many years and in doing so will accrue a history and identity of its own far in excess of that the original SAMSON was able to achieve during its short working life in County Durham. This summary may lead those who have reached this concluding chapter to ask what became of the original SAMSON?

The author has an unwritten rule when trying to fill the gaps in the history of exhibits at Beamish, or add to their historical record, that making an assured and certain statement will very often bring contradictions and counter-arguments. Where these can be substantiated with evidence, the historical record becomes so much the richer and the gaps become a little narrower. So it

is perhaps inevitable that having so certainly stated that there is only one known photograph of SAMSON at Cornish Hush, and that it met its ultimate fate in 1904, some piece of evidence will emerge to challenge this – and it is most certainly hoped that this will be the case! Discovering the remains of the original must be considered highly improbable, but perhaps unearthing an additional photograph is less far-fetched – future editions of this book will depend on such an occurrence.

But why the confidence regarding the date 1904? This is in fact the date of a consignment note for a 'Lewin locomotive' known to have existed, being dispatched for scrap from the North Eastern Railway's Middleton-in-Teesdale station goods yard. This is almost certainly SAMSON, or its remains. It may reflect an even shorter working life for the engine however, as the London Lead Company had surrendered its leases on Cornish Hush in 1883. The company

Above, left & right: The following day, chasing a very tight deadline for the engine to appear in light steam at the April 2016 Great War Steam Fair, SAMSON was loaded onto a Brimec lorry (whose deck tilts and slides) to be moved to the narrow gauge railway. It looked stunning in the spring sunshine – never to be this clean again!

workshops were in Middleton-in-Teesdale and so it would seem very probable that SAMSON was transferred there – but was this upon cessation of mining at Cornish Hush or at an even earlier date?

Entering the realm of speculation, it is possible that SAMSON, with its flywheel and simple construction, might have found use as a stationary engine in the twilight of its life. The very similar HOPS and MALT at the Guinness Brewery in Dublin were found to be unsuited to haulage duties (being unsprung and relatively heavy) but did find favour as portable engines i.e. they could be taken to a place of work where they would be parked and then act as a static power source for whatever process required it. Perhaps SAMSON met the same fate?

The original SAMSON's performance characteristics must also remain speculative, but as further locomotives of this type were built by Stephen Lewin, and that the company trumpeted the construction and sale of this engine so enthusiastically, it must be assumed that it worked to at least a satisfactory degree. Quite how well it was suited to the lightly constructed and previously horse-operated tramway from Cornish Hush will remain unknown. Similarly, how it was reacted to by those whose charge it was put into (presumably in place of their horses) will remain forever obscure. It is entirely possible that once the photograph was captured, SAMSON saw very little use as continuation of horse power due to a conservative nature amongst the miners prevailed, or its unsuitability on the T section rails used on the tramway became apparent.

Alternatively, it may have been a tremendous success and as a result it could have quickly worn out. Experience with No.18 (the Seaham loco) reveal that Stephen Lewin built their locomotives

cheaply and insubstantially – perhaps SAMSON simply wore out? This might explain why it did not find a purchaser when the tramway was closed, nor do the London Lead Company appear to have made any attempt to sell it on.

One last dramatic hypothesis is that it was damaged in an accident, beyond economic or effective repair. The local press of the day are not silent on accidents in the dale however, and examples of reporting of those occurring to riders of waggons on the incline(s) at Bollihope suggest a lurid interest in anything traumatic, so it would be unlikely that SAMSON would have met a spectacular demise. However, damage caused by mishandling such as a low-water incident damaging the firebox would not make good copy and would also prove to be terminal in the wilds of the north Pennines.

It is almost certain that the questions posed above will never be answered, but what can be observed is the performance of the new SAMSON, to whom these closing remarks now turn.

Finally, even in writing the text for this book, each image and piece of evidence has come under renewed scrutiny and so raised the slightly uncomfortable thought that something might have been missed and that the new SAMSON is not quite what it should have been! Fortunately this did not occur but it proved to be an interesting experience, having become so familiar with the new locomotive. Had it proved to be the case that something was missed, no sleep would have been lost as there has always been a clear understanding that this was a new SAMSON, and not, nor could be, an exact facsimile of the original. Should another be built (not impossible, though it would be for another organisation), would it bear the same name, or perhaps it would take on the female role in the partnership and be named DELILAH? Time will tell…

Left: David lights the first fire in the completed locomotive. It was to make one trial run, for our own curiosity, and then would be parked up, its approval thus far only being as a static locomotive. This was due to the very tight deadline set and the need to carry out extensive running trials and commissioning before being presented to the operational department for acceptance.

Below: SAMSON makes one of its first runs under its own power, the sun by now having deserted the occasion! It displayed a certain hesitance to move in both directions, but was certainly capable of driving back and forth and so proved, for a very first attempt, to be a successful start to its operating career and a great moment for David in creating it.

Above: The water tanks were kept as full as possible as there was a very marked tendency for the front end of the locomotive to lift, partly the action of the gears but more so when two people were stood on the footplate! The need to weight the front end had been anticipated and such experimentation would form part of the running trials.

Right: David recreates something of the photograph that started the project off, the right hand side view, square on and reflecting the light across the top of the boiler (achieved by use of a polarising filter on the camera).

Above: Another view of SAMSON *as pressure was built up ahead of another test run before it was placed on display for the four-day Great War Steam Fair.*

Left: For its first four days in the public spotlight, SAMSON *was kept in light steam on an isolated siding, the flywheel ticking over and allowing adjustments to be made and a certain amount of running-in to be completed. It was also a chance for David to talk to the many visitors who came to see the locomotive, many of whom had followed the project on 'the blog' – the author's website for transport news at the Museum: www. beamishtransportonline.co.uk*

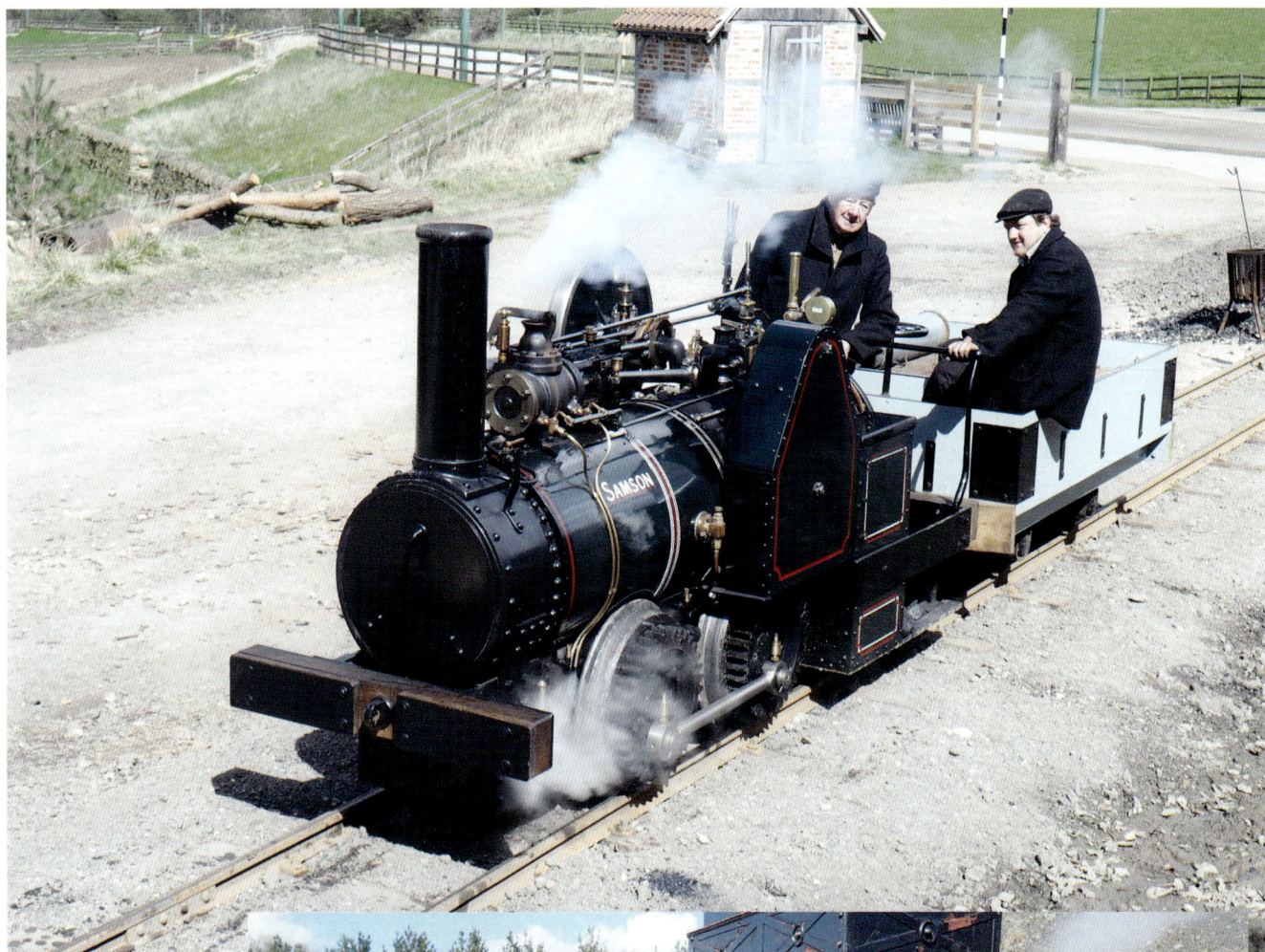

The photographs on these pages show the first full day trial of Samson at Beamish, when it was able to demonstrate some of its prowess on the narrow gauge railway, including dealing with gradients, curves and a modest train. With the sun shining it was also an opportunity to capture a number of the images for this book!

Testing Samson revealed a number of things. One was a breathlessness when working hard, another was the lightness of the front end, causing the locomotive to bounce fairly spectacularly when it hit rail joints or was under particular load (exacerbated by the inclination of the first shaft pinion to 'wind' around the second shaft gear and further raise the front end).

To investigate the former, two pressure gauges were rigged to measure steam chest pressure and exhaust pressure (see photo left). Some modifications were made to the exhaust side of the slide valve, much improving the performance. To assist with the bouncing, 150kg of weight was added to the front frame stretcher, settling this particular tendency down.

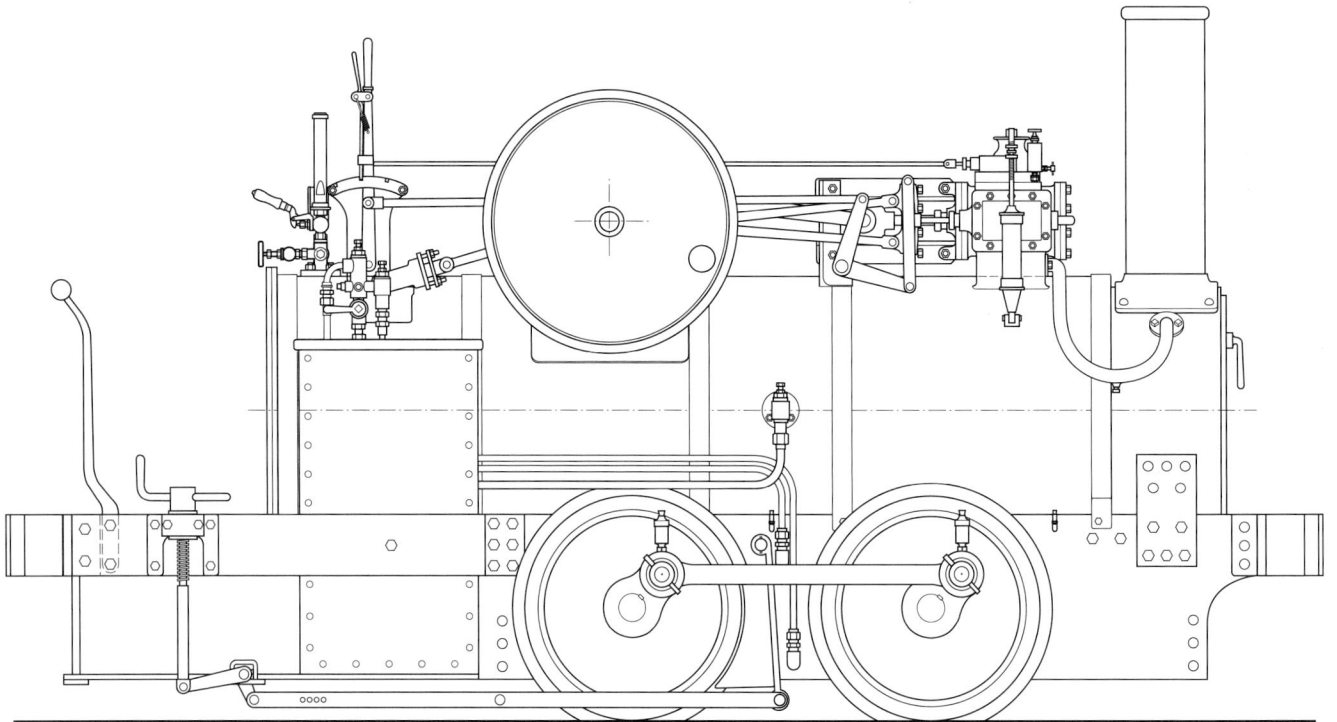

Right Hand Elevation

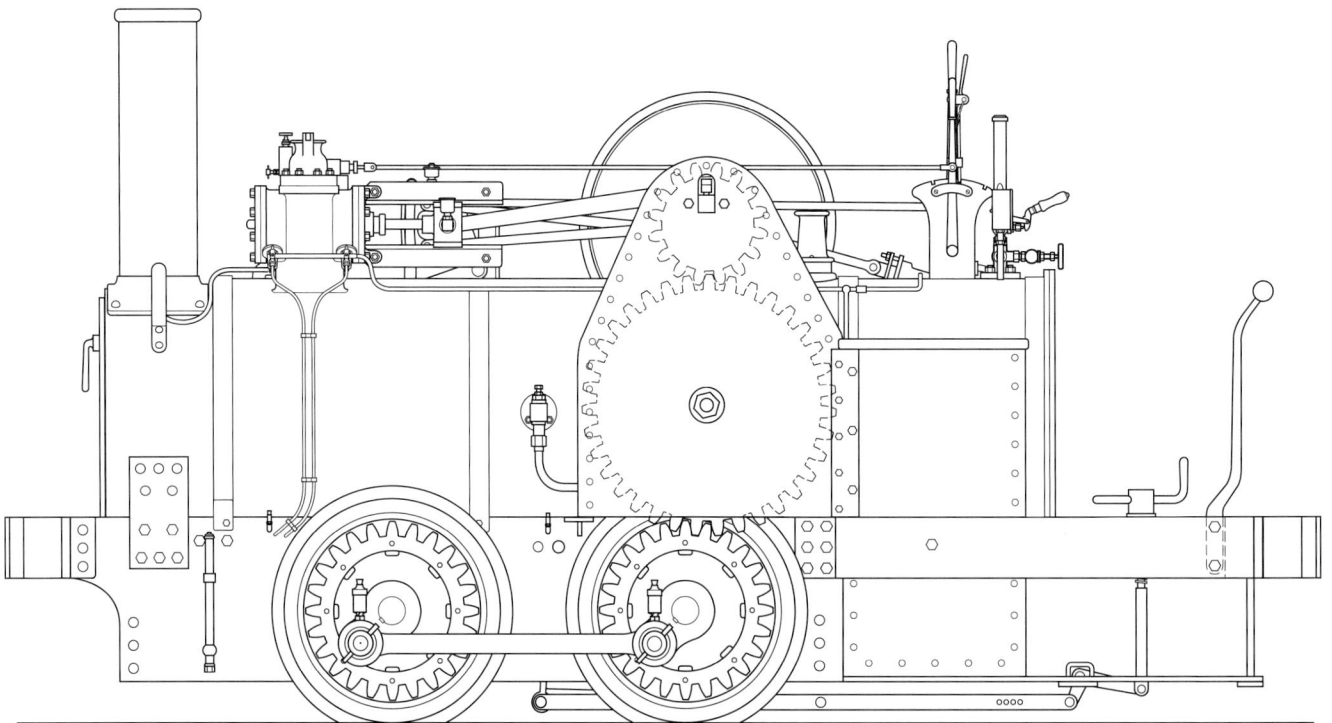

12ins   0   1   2 Feet

Left Hand Elevation

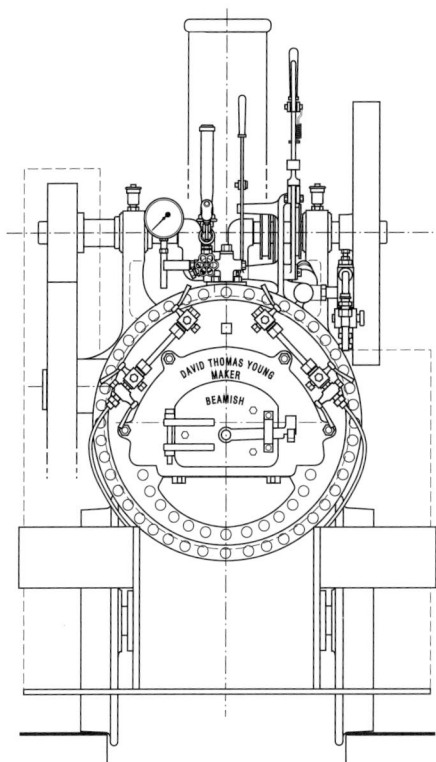

Section looking on to backhead

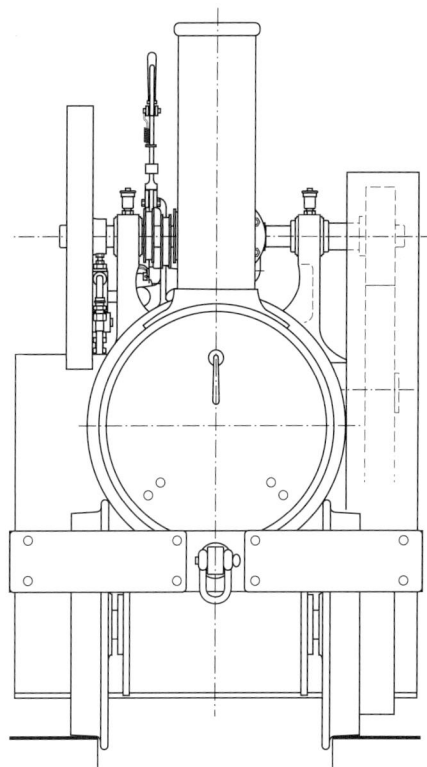

Front Elevation

Samson

NOTES:

New design adapted to 2ft gauge – original was 1ft 10ins gauge.

The engineering drawings elesewhere in this book provide futher detail regarding the design and components – though note some were modified as the build progressed.

Brake block to rear axle on RH side only.

Gearing shown in LH elevation for representation only.

These drawings represent the new locomotive – and have been developed from the proposal diagrams, plus site measurements and photographs taken as the new locomotive was being built.

Note, not all details are shown in all elevations. These drawings must be read in conjuction with photographs.

Scale – 16mm : 1 foot

©Roy C Link May 2016

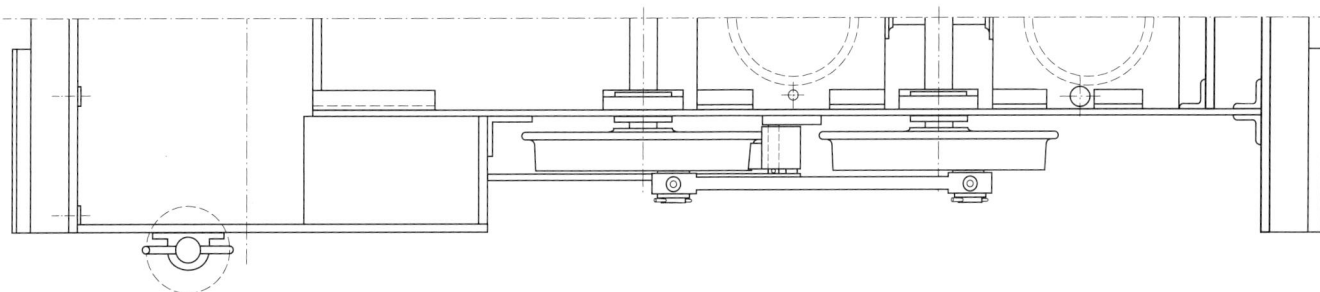

Plan view of Chassis

CHAPTER 11
THE PROJECT SCOPE BROADENS

Above: Taken at Rampgill Mine at Nenthead, a compact area of intensive lead mining and still fascinating for the industrial archaeologist today. The waggons are being loaded with waste from the mine tips, this being taken for dressing and use in building. The photograph is dated around 1910 and shows the versatility of these waggons even after the mines they worked in had been closed.

FROM THE BEGINNING of this project there was a concern that SAMSON's water capacity would be extremely limited. Knowing that with this particular locomotive there might be a tendency to run it at a fairly low pressure (compared to the potential pressure of the boiler) then water consumption was expected to be reasonably high. Also, with a by-pass pump being fitted, there was a likelihood that the feed water supply in the tank could warm up when circulating and so cause a failure of the injector (which requires cold water to correctly function). It was therefore decided that whilst a tender for SAMSON would not be invented, a lead tub of appropriate design would be useful to carry an additional (cold) water supply.

LONDON LEAD COMPANY WAGGONS
Within the collection at Beamish were two London Lead Company bottom discharge tubs. One was more or less complete whilst the other was in derelict condition. With the former as the 'type specimen' the latter was selected for reconstruction and adaptation for operation with SAMSON. Replicas of this type of waggon were

Right: This view is charming for the detail not only of the waggons, but also the narrow horse-shaped adit mouths seen commonly in the lead mining industry. Taken at Skears Low Level, Hudshope Burn in Teesdale, this was a London Lead Company mine driven in 1821 and penetrating 4625 feet into the vein This gives a very clear idea of what the adit mouth at Cornish Hush would have looked like. Note the waggon buffers do not touch, despite the tops being in contact. (16588)

Below: Another archive view, again taken at Nenthead but this time at Smallcleugh Mine (still regularly explored today and famous for its 'Ball Room' cavern deep within the workings). Just visible to the right of the large white building is a pony leading a rake of waggons into the mine. The brutal, lunar landscape is easily appreciated, and remains similar today, heavily poisoned by the industry that is inextricably linked to this particular location.

Above: This waggon is retained in the Beamish collection as the 'type specimen', this meaning that it is retained in unrestored and totally original condition as a reference piece, unrestored and unmodified. Page opposite: The waggon used for SAMSON's 'tender' was recovered from deep in the Museum's outside stores, providing little more than a pattern and some iron components.

built for lead mining museum at Killhope in the 1980s (which was actually operated by another company not using this type of waggon) and a cast iron wheel blank was available to borrow in order for a new set to be cast for the 'tender'. The original wheels were not suitable for reuse due to their thin flanges and wooden inserts to secure the wheels themselves onto their axles.

These waggons were distinctive in both their outline and their construction. A timber chassis was integral with side frames of the same material (Douglas Fir on the reconstructed waggon) and this had side and end plates of iron within this frame – components that were saved and reused from the derelict waggon. The style of waggon (made entirely of wood) probably originated in the 18th century, with the iron plated waggons appearing from the early 1800s, the cast iron wheelsets being timber wedged onto square ended axles and running in open grease bearings fixed to the underside of the chassis members. An iron door enabled discharge from the bottom of the waggon (an early hopper in this regard) and iron tie-bars were

used to add strength and secure components together. Of particular interest are the side mounted wrought-iron drawbars, ideally suited to horse drawing on the surface and clear of the manpower used underground.

One unusual feature is that the waggons are fitted with simple buffers, but the length of the body over the top rails extends beyond these buffers, so that two waggons coupled together will not touch buffer to buffer. On the rebuilt waggon the bottom rails were extended in order for the buffers to function in a conventional manner, and a drawbar and simple hook and link couplings were made and fitted to the underside of the waggon, the need to discharge a load no longer being applicable. A water tank is carried inside the waggon, raised above the level of the water tanks on SAMSON to aid filling them. Additional coal and tools can also be carried when needed.

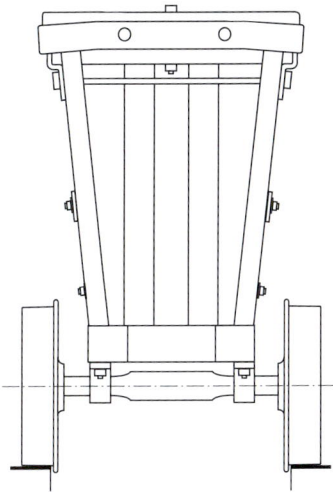

A TENDER FOR SAMSON

12ins   0   1   2 Feet

Scale – 16mm : 1 foot

©Roy C Link May 2016

The rebuilt waggon has re-gauged wheelsets, Extended frames are fitted, with revised buffing faces, as mentioned in the text (see plan view right), which are compatible with Samson and enable them to function in the conventional sense. The waggon was rebuilt by Matthew Beddard as his completion of apprenticeship piece in the restoration workshops at Beamish.

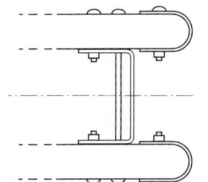

Above: Samson on a trial run, with a brake tender adapted from an ammunition wagon.

Left: Further practical experience suggested that additional coal capacity and tool stowage would be useful and to this end the ex Horwich 18in. gauge tender behind Wren in the National Railway Museum has been surveyed and will form a follow-on project to Samson's construction, once again enjoying David Young's input into its construction.

A NEW ENGINE SHED FOR SAMSON

Whilst the narrow gauge railway at Beamish is operated as frequently as possible, this presently constitutes two dozen occasions per year. Plans exist to increase this, but it was realised that SAMSON would be of great interest to the Museum's visitors and so placing it on display when not in steam was an important objective. It was also felt that 'another' tin shed on the narrow gauge railway would not match the quality of the contents, so the author turned his eyes towards a building known to him as the subject of a never-quite-started model some years previously.

Crich is located in Derbyshire, best known today as the home of the National Tramway Museum which skirts the limestone quarry which created the requirement for a mineral railway to the lime kilns at Ambergate a few miles to the south. George Stephenson became the engineer for the North Midland Railway in 1836, and in carrying out excavations for this project he encountered rich coal seams, so rich that he took out leases for coal mining at Clay Cross in 1838. Later he turned his eyes towards the limestone outcrop at Crich and the potential for lime kilns to be constructed at Ambergate. The route combined a gently graded tramway terminating in a steep rope worked incline – sound familiar?

Initially horse operated; in 1893 steam locomotive power was introduced along with the formal, and very unusual for the United Kingdom, gauge of one metre. To house the first steam locomotive, the stable at Chadwick Nick, part way along the route, was adapted for its new role, including provision of a large doorway and a water supply to an adjacent tank. The railway closed in 1957 and the rails were later lifted and used on the Talyllyn Railway as it

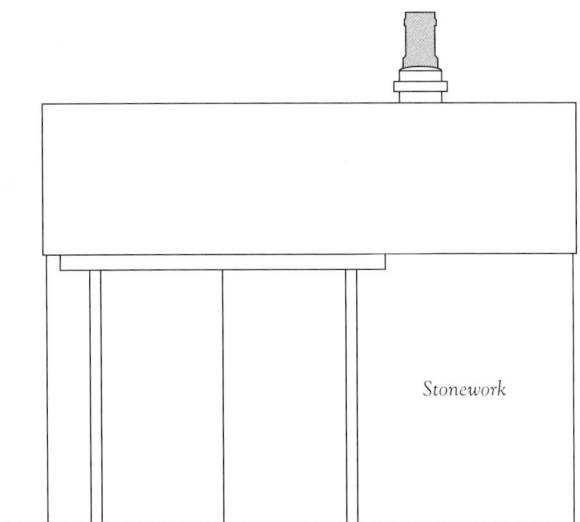

Door Elevation

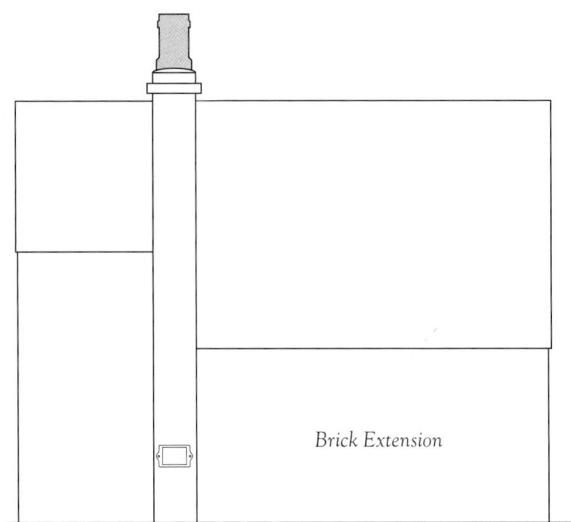

Rear Elevation

PROPOSED ENGINE SHED FOR SAMSON

Based on a structure at Chadwick Nick (Crich) and adapted to suit Samson – so the locomotive can be exhibited to the public when not in use.

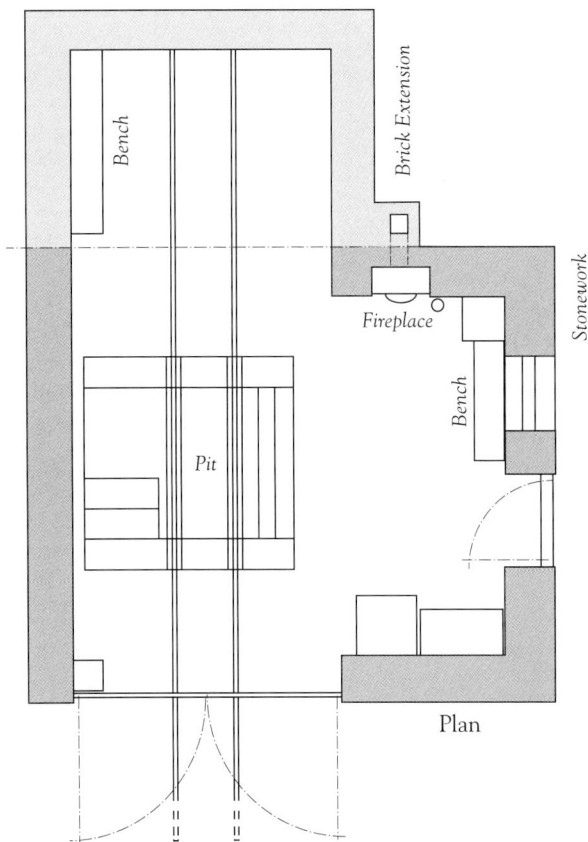

Stonework

Brick Extension

Bench

Brick Extension

Fireplace

Stonework

Bench

Pit

Plan

Stonework

Brick Extension

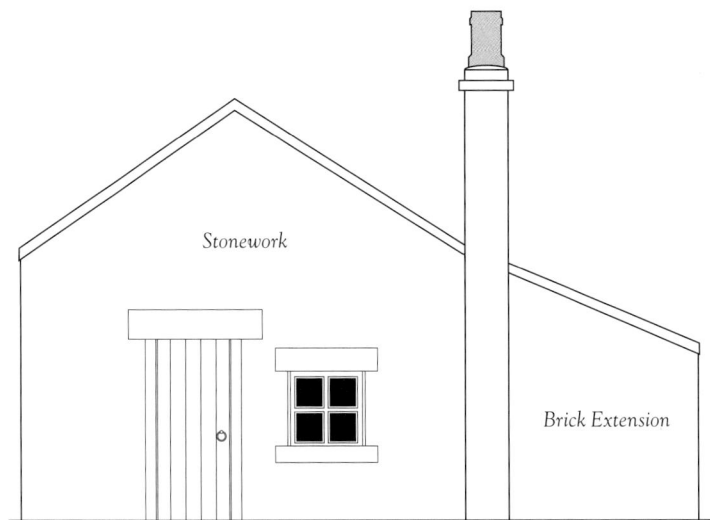

Side Elevation

12ins 1   12 Feet

Scale – 4mm : 1 foot
©Paul Jarman May 2016

struggled out of operational dereliction into the fine railway it is today. Amazingly, the engine shed at Chadwick Nick survived and remains in remarkably intact condition, such that a rough set of drawings had been made by the author some time before the idea of building it in full size was conceived.

It may seem incongruous to build a slightly modified replica of a building from Derbyshire in County Durham, but its construction embodied the north east vernacular style, with substantial walls supporting a pantile and stone roof. The shed will be complete with a pit, fireplace and the trappings of SAMSON's life as it might have been a century plus ago, and will make a fitting residence for the locomotive as well as an attractive exhibit for visitors to Beamish to enjoy.

CHAPTER 12

WHAT REMAINS OF THE OTHER TRAMWAYS?

IN CHAPTER TWO the Cornish Hush Tramway was explored in considerable detail, whilst in Chapter 5 three other steam-worked narrow gauge tramways were examined. It is to these that this closing chapter now returns, to compare the past views with the present.

The site at Stanhopeburn had a varied history, its final incarnation being associated with fluorspar prospecting by SAMUK as late as the 1982. By this date additional buildings had been constructed and the former blacksmith shop, seen in the photo on Page 38, was converted to house a battery electric locomotive.

The view above shows a comparable one to that seen earlier, looking into the area where ore was tipped, revealing remarkably little change other than the inevitable decay of such a site.

Above: This is the blacksmiths shop, which sits immediately adjacent to the adit mouth at Stanhopeburn and which was adapted in the 1970s to house a battery electric locomotive. The rails for this are just visible protruding from the doorway. This shed was never used by LITTLE SALLY when that locomotive was in operation over the tramway, and the later railway operation would appear to have been confined to this area and its immediate environs, the route of the tramway itself being converted to a road.

Left: Whilst the route along the Stanhopeburn Valley is largely cut into the northerly hillside, the tramway took a straighter course than the burn and on one short stretch it penetrated a bluff in the natural stone, requiring this section of stone walling. Despite the inevitable disturbance by vegetation and trees, the walls remain in relatively good condition.

Page opposite upper: The route of the tramway at Stanhopeburn is now a roadway, well used by walkers, cyclists and horse riders. This scene contrasts with that shown on Page 38, the standard gauge origins of the formation remaining evident, though the tree growth appears surprisingly restrained.

Page opposite lower: Very little of the Wolfcleugh or Boltsburn tramway routes remain intact today, but remains of the smelting mill at Rookhope still stand to identify the site as a central industrial location in the area. The arch is a fragment of a series of arches, which carried the flue from the hearths at the mill, over the burn, road and railway and on up the adjacent hillside, LITTLE NUT's railway ran on the far side of the burn, with the area of Boltsburn being located in the left hand distance of this view.

APPENDICES

APPENDIX 1 – THE STORY OF A DETERMINED MAN
– A SHORT AUTOBIOGRAPHY OF DAVID THOMAS YOUNG

I WAS BORN ONE OF TWINS, a little prior to World War 2 when there was little of the wealth seen today and as a general rule if you wanted something you had to make it. This was encouraged in the teaching in schools of such subjects as woodwork, metalwork and gardening but as with all disciplines the earlier you started to learn a skill the more natural it later became. Our maternal grandparents had a building and contracting business and although curtailed for the duration of the war we were mixing cement at an early age!

Woodwork in the form of model boat building was an early activity but working with metal became a much more challenging skill. At its most basic level we learned to file straight and true in an old air-raid shelter with candles for illumination.

At this time there were handguns just about everywhere and among my small collection of tools was a five chambered F.N. Revolver which I well recall carrying to school on the bus! Although we attended a good school there was a need for a supply of gunpowder for the making of small cannon guns and we entered the manufacturing industry of both, safely but with many lessons learned the hard way. This led to the purchase of a treadle driven screw cutting lathe and we progressed into model loco building and the guns were disposed of…

Looking back this development is not so surprising as our paternal grandparents and relations were all connected with local railway engineering. Our grandfather, a blacksmith for Lambton Collieries told us from an early age that his grandfather, Thomas Young, had been Foreman at South Hetton Colliery workshops and had supervised the conversion or restoration of the Hetton No.2 locomotive. On

A youthful David poses in the cockpit of his 1929 Riley 9 'Special'.

many occasions grandfather reminded me that his grandfather's words were "everyone thinks it is the Hetton No.1 but I know it is the Hetton No2!".

Several other members of the family were involved in activities at the Lambton Engine Works at Philadelphia so perhaps my enthusiasm is in the blood.

I was fortunate to obtain a place in the drawing office of the Washington Chemical Co and served an apprenticeship as a draughtsman and surveyor remaining there for 17 years, except for two years National Service in the RAF.

After demob, by the greatest stroke of luck I met and married Maureen, my wife now for over 50 years and with new confidence I obtained employment with the N.C.B. in their coke oven division.

At this time vintage cars could be had cheaply and, encouraged by a near neighbour who owned a Hispano Suiza, I started to buy and eventually run a series of old cars. All needed much work and included a 1934 Rolls Royce which needed two years' work before it would run. It was a project from which I learned about the best in engineering standards which had been

An early machine shop, set up in the garden, was housed in the teak and brass wheelhouse obtained for £40 and removed from the tanker San Valerio (built at Palmers Shipyard in Jarrow in 1913 and broken up in Sunderland in 1953, being used as a gatehouse thereafter until 1978). This was subsequently extended using an additional wheelhouse, the pair later being sold on.

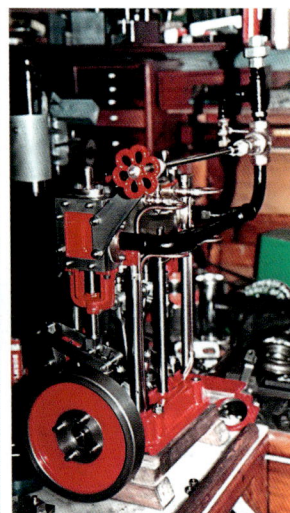

Above left: VALHALLA (built in 1986), David's steam launch, was completed in just three and a half years and gave many years of pleasure to David, his family and friends. Seen here on Ullswater, it was later sold and moved to Switzerland and now lives on Lake Brienz. Above centre: The steam engine built by David for VALHALLA was a Taylor twin cylinder vertical launch engine built from commercially available castings and developing 2.5 hp. It is fitted with Stephenson valve gear. Above right: The engine and boiler in situ within the hull of VALHALLA. The boiler is of the water tube type and has a working pressure of 120psi (8.5 bar).

my main objective. Other cars followed including a nice Alvis tourer but I then hankered after something steam driven.

Experience with various steam driven plant at the coke works, probably the last commercial use of steam, led to the building of a steam launch.

This was 21 ft long with a water tube boiler and a two-cylinder engine and after over three years work Maureen launched it on the River Wear naming her VALHALLA. I chose the name because it was easy to cut out from brass!

With this boat I could enjoy steam with my wife, our daughter Victoria and our good friends, an activity I thoroughly recommend.

Eventually it all ran its course, I left the Coal Board after the miners strike and, as a Safety Engineer took on assorted jobs including lecturing, accident investigating and even two years in a shipyard, all valuable experience.

In 2006 having been retired six years I returned to an old passion, Beamish Museum. Here I made the acquaintance of my dear friend Paul Jarman which led to me working as a volunteer. In this capacity I was heavily involved with the restoration of the locomotives COFFEE POT and 'Lewin' [No.18] and built a small portable steam engine known as the STEAM MULE.

To bring the saga up to date I have almost completed the building of the replica narrow gauge loco SAMSON. So now at the age of 78, with my beloved wife and family, two fine grandsons who are showing great talent and still in fair health, what is next?

Above: Maureen Young launches VALHALLA at Fatfield on the River Wear, once the location of river staithes for shipping coal from the Durham coalfield, at one time, the largest in the world.

David's working models of a Marshall portable engine and Fowler B5 traction engine, the latter being completed in around 14 years work across a 22 year period – building steam launches getting in the way for a number of years!

APPENDIX 2 – WHERE DOES THE INSPIRATION COME FROM?

MOST AUTHORS WILL have particular writers that have inspired or given impetus to their own work, and I will confine my references here to three, though there could be a great many more…

Firstly, the writings of L. T. C. Rolt have never failed to awaken in me the enthusiasm for our industrial history and in particular those branches which so well reflected the obsessive quality of mankind to produce machines that go way beyond form and function and so serve to placate the artistic elements of the mind, with objects that appeal in ways beyond that of their mechanical accomplishment and ingenuity. Our SAMSON, whilst functional, manages to satisfy such whims, and an example of this was the beautiful cast iron fluted trumpet to conceal the modern safety valve. This was inspired by some of the drawings which illustrate my second reference, that seminal work by Alfred Rosling Bennet – *The Chronicles of Boulton's Siding*.

Isaac Watt Boulton's engines were a wonderful example of mechanical bricolage and the variety of manufacturers' products that passed through Boulton's hands, often rebuilt or combined into new forms, set this dealer aside as notable in giving life to locomotives way beyond what they might have justifiably felt entitled to. The drawings in this book show locomotives of great interest, but the details of each are truly revealing of that era of locomotive design and construction that is very poorly represented in material form today. It was from a number of these illustrations to what is one of the most beautifully written books that I have read that the safety valve cover was extracted and so ably replicated by David for the new SAMSON.

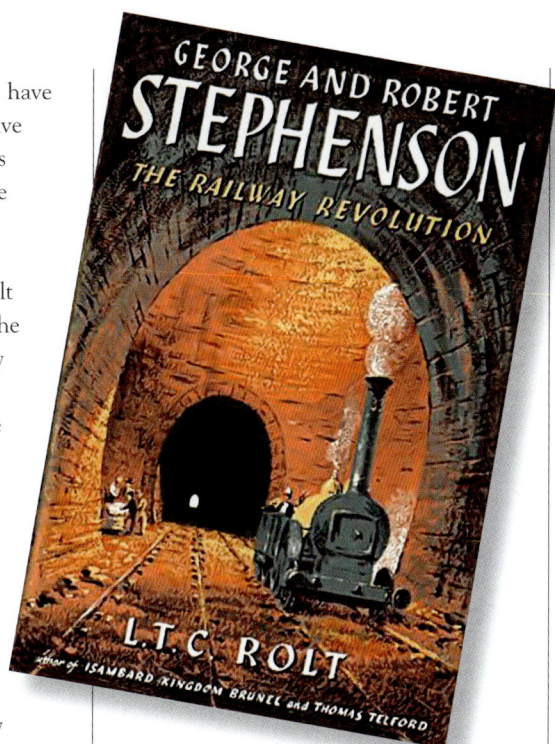

The third book of inspiration here is that edited by Charles Lee and which brought to an audience the autobiography of George Hardy, the engineer who took the Londonderry Railway in County Durham from a piteous assemblage of unsuitable second-hand motive power to a railway with workshops capable of building fine steam engines (and road steam waggons), many of which would endure under later North Eastern Railway ownership. His efforts to 'create' a working lathe with which to equip his embryonic works are heroic, and this tenacity paid off in the years that followed. A book which inspires you to go out and work hard! If a fourth title was permitted, it would be Alan Bloom's *Steam Engines at Bressingham* – truly illustrating what can be accomplished if one puts mind, heart and soul into a project.

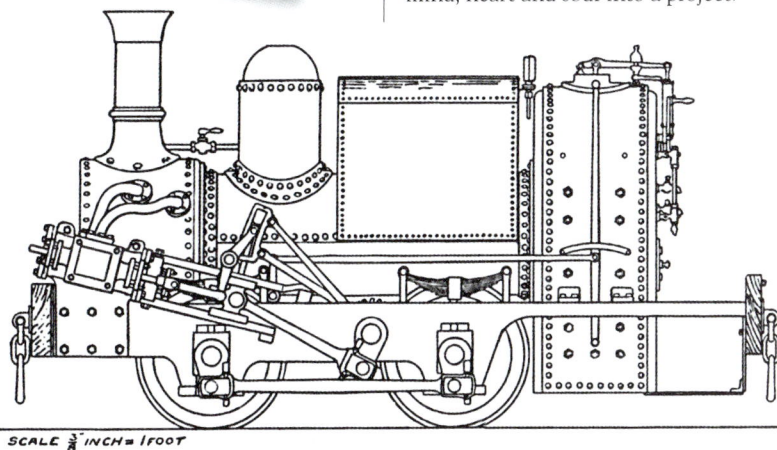

SCALE 3/8 INCH = 1 FOOT

First published as a series of articles in **The Locomotive** *magazine in the early to mid 1920's with the title* **The Chronicles of Boulton's Sidings** *– written by Alfred Rosling Bennett. In 1926 they were gathered together to make a book of the same title. This was subsequently re-printed in 1971, by David & Charles, with addtional material, plus an index.*

It is a remarkable document, detailing contractors locomotives from a past long gone. LITTLE GRIMSBY, was one such. Originally built as a standard gauge loco circa 1856, for work on a coke-oven contract. When this ended in 1861, the loco was rebuilt to suit 2ft gauge (see above) – something that took a good deal of alteration. Such was the interest at the time, that Zerah Colburn made reference to her in his notable work **Locomotive Engineering and Mechanism of Railways**. *This was, remember, prior to the introduction of steam power on the Festiniog Railway in 1863. In 1864 Boulton took the loco back in stock again, this time regauging to 2ft 8ins, a simpler task than the earlier conversion, requiring little more than longer axles. This time the loco was sent out to the Weardale Iron & Coal Company. Here she worked out her final years and was finally scrapped.*

APPENDIX 3 – SAMSON AND THE MODERN SAFETY MANAGEMENT SYSTEM

AS SAMSON IS A new locomotive, consideration of responsibilities under ROGS (Rail and Other Guided Systems) have to be given. Pre-ROGS the HMRI (Her Majesty's Railway Inspectorate) would have been contacted at the beginning of the project and they would have overseen the creation of what is essentially a new locomotive design until final sign-off as fit for purpose. However, now the onus is on the builder (so in this case it would be Beamish) to ensure that the design is fit for purpose. Where risk is changed markedly from existing operation, an ICP (Independent Competent Person) should be appointed. In the case of the boiler design, this would be undertaken by a qualified and indemnified engineer (Graham Morris) and approved by a notified body (an appropriately competent insurance company – Royal Sun Alliance in this case).

It was determined at this stage that as SAMSON is essentially a traction engine, operating on a railway, the risk presented is not notably at variance with Beamish's existing operation of a wide variety of steam traction on road, rail and stationary. Therefore an ICP would not be appointed, though Matt Ellis, Keeper of Transport, had arrived at Beamish once the project was well established and, by remaining detached from the construction phases, was able to bring an independent eye and considerable experience to bear in the commissioning of SAMSON for operation at the Museum.

The boiler design, once approved, enabled components to be ordered. These were then prepared at Beamish before final assembly (assisted by Beamish staff) was carried out by the Severn Valley Railway, who affixed their CE marked conformity plate to the boiler once the steam test had been carried out.

Once the construction phase was complete and the steam test accomplished, a phase of testing began. Final painting was also carried out at this stage. Running in of the engine, whilst the locomotive was stationary, was done within the workshop complex of the RHEC (Regional Heritage Engineering Centre) to enable any remedial work to be readily carried out. It was then moved to the narrow gauge railway at Beamish for further test running before it was presented to the operations team for a full Fitness To Run (FTR) examination by the Keeper of Transport and Steam Technician.

The author provided training, holding existing competencies for both road steam and rail steam traction at the Museum. It was then down to a final acceptance examination and sign-off as a complete and fit locomotive available for traffic. Training of crews will always be ongoing, but knowledge of a single cylinder traction engine or steam roller is certainly advantageous when handling SAMSON, its single cylinder leading to an increased tendency of 'stopping on its centres' (despite Stephen Lewin's advertising claims in 1874…).

APPENDIX 4 – A THORNY QUESTION – WHAT COLOUR WAS SAMSON?

UNTIL THE DAY THAT science can provide a means of detecting colour from a black and white image, historians can only speculate as to the colour SAMSON was painted. If it is assumed that it is very nearly new in the photograph (as the hard life and exposure to the elements of even a few working years at Cornish Hush would surely manifest themselves in the image), it can be observed that the engine is a relatively dark shade with a simple pin striping on top of this. Whilst the shade appears dark, the potential for the chemicals used in the photographic process to create a misleading shade is becoming well understood, with orthochromatic chemicals being blind to some colours, such as red (and derivatives of) and therefore rendering negatives clear. The result of developing and printing these is thus a dark shade, not at all representative of the original colour photographed. Therefore, by this application of logic, SAMSON could be a bright red colour, although the observer would usually suggest that it is green or even black.

The appearance of the pin striping (which appears in one engraving on the gear case and in the other engraving on the bunker sides) could also mislead, again the observer might suggest it is red, but again it could be an element of the red spectrum and therefore, theoretically, could be a red or yellow line on a red or brown base colour.

As the best 'hunch' was that the locomotive was green, a very dark shade was selected, reminiscent of the Cambrian

Railway's 'Invisible Green' (which appears to be black to most observers). The effect is to mirror the uncertainty of the original photograph in the appearance of the new SAMSON in that in some lights it appears black; in brighter lights it is green! The lining style was selected to define the shape of the locomotive and was based on that carried by the two Stephen Lewin locomotives supplied to the Guinness Brewery and for which a photograph and contemporary engraving exist. A deep crimson line with inverted corners is balanced by an off-white line set behind it. It was felt that this created a reasonable compromise and also reflected what was more typical of Stephen Lewin's paint finishes when first applied.

To test out the chosen colour scheme, a panel was made up to show each key feature, based on the dark green background. This also included a section showing the stages of painting, a sample boiler band and a the locomotive's name. The measurements on this panel, such as for indents or curves, are all definitive and have been used on the new SAMSON when applying the paintwork and lining.

APPENDIX 5 – WHERE DID THE NAME COME FROM?

THE LOCOMOTIVE THAT worked at Cornish Hush, and the one built at Beamish, both carry the name SAMSON more in association than through formal attachment. It might well be imagined that such a tiny locomotive arriving in the dales in 1874 might have a rather unkind moniker attached to it – there is certainly no evidence of a formal naming or, indeed, any name at all being carried. Similarly, Beamish's new SAMSON has carried the name through association with the original and again because it so aptly reflects everything the little engine isn't! There is a little more intrigue on the subject however.

Alan Myers, author of *Myer's Literary Guide: The North East* wrote a letter to the W. H. Auden Society which appeared in their April 1996 Newsletter No.14 suggesting that the poet and writer's character 'Sampson' in his poem 'In the

year of my youth…' was named after the locomotive which had worked for the London Lead Company at Cornish Hush. Auden did have connections with the area, drawing inspiration from the declining lead mining industry in the dales and writing of the places he visited, including those in his 1932 poem.

Whether or not this is true it is an interesting matter of conjecture not least for the spelling of the name as Sampson. This takes the form of a not uncommon surname and even a character in Shakespeare's 'Romeo and Juliet' (one of the Capulet servants). However, the conventional spelling of the biblical character of supernatural strength is Samson, so if the name was applied ironically to the steam locomotive, it would seem more likely to be biblically derived rather than from Shakespearean literature…

APPENDIX 6 – MAIN TECHNICAL DETAILS

GENERAL DIMENSIONS	DIMENSION	NOTES
Whyte notation	0-4-0WTG	
Length	10 ft 9½ ins	
Width	3 ft 6 ins	
Height	5 ft 10 ins	
Weight	2 tons 12 cwt	Based on original locomotive details
MECHANICAL PARTICULARS		
Driving Wheel diameter	22 ins	
Flywheel diameter	26 ins	
First shaft PCD	7½ ins	
Second Shaft PCD	23½ ins	
Gear ring PCD	17½ ins	
Gear ratio (overall)	1 : 2·25	
Wheelbase	2 ft 6 ins	
Cylinder diameter	4¾ ins	
Cylinder stroke	7 ins	
BOILER DIMENSIONS		
Barrel length	8 ft	
Barrel diameter	2 ft	
Firebox length	2 ft 6 ins	
Firebox diameter	1 ft 4 ins	
Tubes – number of	37	
Tubes - diameter	1⁹⁄₁₆ ins	
Boiler pressure (design)	160psi	Normal operating pressure 120psi
OTHER DETAILS		
Gauge of original locomotive	1 ft 10in	
Gauge of new locomotive	2 ft	
Power of new locomotive	13.274 bhp	$\dfrac{\text{(Pressure x Piston area x RPM)}}{33000}$

APPENDIX 7 – BOILER COMPONENTS

COMPONENT	MATERIAL	MATERIAL SPEC
Boiler Barrel	9.5mm steel tube	ASTM A106 Grade B
Firebox tube	9.5mm steel tube	ASTM A106 Grade B
Backhead	16mm Boiler Plate	BS EN10028-2 P265GH (BS1501-151/161-430B)
Smokebox Tubeplate	16mm Boiler Plate	BS EN10028-2 P265GH (BS1501-151/161-430B)
Firebox Tubeplate	12.5mm Boiler Plate	BS EN10028-2 P265GH (BS1501-151/161-430B)
Barrel angle ring	150mm x 150mm x 15mm Mild Steel	BS EN1005:S275 (BS4360 43A)
Expansion brackets	1.5 inch square Mild Steel	BS970:070M20 (En3B) or BS970:080M15 (En32B)
Firebox side stays	Monel (Nickel Copper)	BS3076 NA13
Boiler tubes	Boiler Tube	BS3059:ERW/HFS320 or BS3602 CFS360
Rivets (throughout)	Steel (Hot formed)	BS425 BS EN10025:S275 (BS4360 43A)
Bushes and pads	Mild Steel (as required)	BS970:070M20 (En3B) or BS970:080M15 (En32B)
Studs, bolts and nipples	Mild Steel (as required)	BS970:070M20 (En3B) or BS970:080M15 (En32B)
Cylinder block casting	SG Iron (various blanks)	SG Iron
Fusible Plug	Gunmetal	BS 1123:2006
Boiler Washout Plug	Gunmetal	LG4
Pressure Gauge	N/A	Calibration Certificate 342029 EN837
Salter Spring Balance	Gunmetal (various blanks)	BS 1400 LG2
Pop Safety Valve	N/A	
Water gauge fittings	Gunmetal	BS 1400-LG2C

REFERENCES

Fairbairn, R. A.
British Mining No.54: Lead Mine Waggons
(Northern Mines Research Society, 1995)   pp 25 - 26

Fisher, A. Fisher, D. & Pierce Jones, Dr G.
De Winton of Caernarfon – Engineers of Excellence
(Roy C Link Publications, 2011)

Fletcher, J.
Early Locomotives at Swanscombe Cement Works
Archive Magazine 7 (Lightmoor Press, 1995)

Foley, P.
Guinness Brewery Portfolio…
Narrow Gauge and Industrial Railway Modelling Review 61
(RCL Publications, 2005)   pp 206 – 209

Foley, P.
The Aveling & Porter Compound Traction Engine Locomotive
Narrow Gauge and Industrial Railway Modelling Review
(RCL Publications, 2009)   pp 190 – 191

Forbes, I.
Lead and Life at Killhope
(Official guidebook for Killhope Lead Mining Museum)

Guy, A. & Atkinson, F.
West Durham: The Archaeology of Industry
(Chichester, 2008)

Hillier, E. G.
Steam Boiler Construction
(National Boiler and General Insurance Co. Ltd, 1920)

Hutchinson, I. K.
Traction Engine Locomotives
(Road Locomotive Society, 1981) pp 38 – 39

Lowe, D. A. & Bevis, A. W.
A Manual of Machine Drawing and Design
(various editions)

Lowe, J. W.
British Steam Locomotive Builders
(London, 1975)

Mountford, C. E & Holroyde, D.
The Industrial Railways & Locomotives of County Durham Part 1
(Industrial Railway Society, 2006)   pp 229 – 230

Ransom, P. J. G
Narrow Gauge Steam
(OPC, 1996)

Raistrick, A & Roberts,
A Life and Work of the Northern Leadminer
(Alan Sutton/Beamish, 1984)

Smithers, M
Sir Arthur Heywood and the Fifteen Inch Gauge Railway
(Plateway Press, 1995)

Smithers, M
An illustrated history of 18 Inch Gauge Steam Railways
(OPC, 1993)

Smithers, M
Renaissance of a Manx Miget
(Heritage Railway Magazine pp78-80)

Talbot, E. & Taylor, C.
Crewe Works Narrow Gauge System
(London & North Western Railway Society Publication, 2005)

Wear, R. & Lees, E.
Stephen Lewin and the Poole Foundry
(Industrial Railway Society and Industrial
Locomotive Society, 1978)

Anon
Narrow Gauge Locomotives for Shunting at a Brewery
The Locomotive Magazine No.76 Vol VII April 1902, pages 62 – 64

The full construction of SAMSON was recorded on the Beamish Transport Blog – actually a growing website with a regularly updated news thread. This can be accessed at www.beamishtransportonline. co.uk and by looking for the heading SAMSON all of the applicable postings over the last four years can be accessed including links to short films showing stages in the construction and the completed locomotive at work. Beamish Museum has an extensive web-presence including a YouTube channel, where films of interest may also be found.

THE BEAMISH CONNECTION...

THROUGHOUT THIS BOOK, reference has been made to Beamish Museum, the location for SAMSON's construction and the home of the completed locomotive. Perhaps a brief explanation as to what Beamish is and how it came to be formed will be useful for readers to place the locomotive, and this project, into some context.

The idea of forming an open air museum for the north east of England was something that was both sown and germinated under the leadership of the museum's founder and first director, Dr Frank Atkinson. In the late 1950s he was the director of the Bowes Museum, a fine-art collection in Barnard Castle, Co Durham and the tangible evidence of the colossal wealth colliery owners derived from the county in the 18th and 19th centuries.

Frank was inspired by the Swedish folk parks and this led him to begin collecting objects for a projected museum in the north east, though at that time there was no location in mind. The collection grew into one of some scale, including not only domestic items but also artefacts from heavy industry, transport and mining.

It was clear to Frank that an open air museum on the scale he was planning would require the support of the region's local authorities, and so he began to work his magic, eventually creating a Joint Committee of these authorities, from across the north east, and so giving birth to what was to become Beamish – The North of England Open Air Museum (now known to many as simply 'Beamish'), Beamish itself being the most local village.

In 1970 Frank left the Bowes Museum and set up a small staff of four at Beamish Hall, a former NCB office, where the adjacent parkland had been deemed as eminently suitable to the founding of the open air museum that he planned. By 1971 an exhibition about the making of the museum opened at the hall and in parallel work

had begun on the wider site. This led to the opening in 1973 of the first section of electric tramway, running from a depot adjacent to farm buildings and cottages (now the workshops) to an open space where a sign ambitiously announced that it would be the location for a recreated Edwardian town.

It probably does not need much more explanation to confirm that Frank's vision did indeed become a reality and that his belief that an living museum where labels were largely banned and that objects came to life through their demonstration to and engagement with the general public, would be a success.

In 1987 Frank retired, having the satisfaction of receiving the European Museum of the year award on behalf of Beamish. The organisation continues to go from strength to strength and now attracts over 650,000 visitors per annum, has an unrivalled series of attractions within the 400 acre site and hosts a wide variety of events across the calendar including the renowned Great North Festival of Transport.

Against this background, and with internationally significant projects such as the recreation of a working 1820s steam Waggonway, the creation of SAMSON can perhaps be seen in new context.

The building of SAMSON itself came about largely through the investment in workshops and engineering facilities at the museum and which continue to grow and develop even now, under the banner 'Regional Heritage Engineering Centre'.

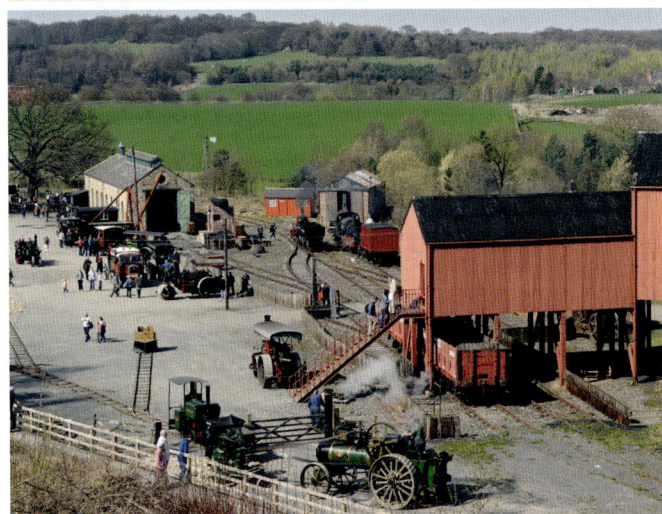

The museum has ambitious plans to expand from 2017, to include a substantial 1950s urban area featuring domestic and urban buildings (including a cinema) as well as a Georgian coaching inn and developments in the 1820s landscape. The railways also benefit from constant development, there being four in total plus the electric tramway; the narrow gauge system around the Colliery area being the latest development and which will allow for realistic pit stockyard shunting operations and footplate rides for visitors.

More can be learned at: www.Beamish.org.uk or: www.beamishtransportonline.co.uk

A Ant 23, 29

Aveling & Porter 27, 33

B Bee 23, 29

Beyer, Peacock 29, 30, 33, 34

Blue Circle 27

Bollihope 1, 3, 6, 9, 10, 16, 104

Boltsburn 39, 40, 41, 42 50, 120

Boulton, Isaac Watt 28, xiii

C Chadwick Nick 117, 118

Clay, Jonathan 43, 44, 50

Clay Cross 117

Coffee Pot No.1 vii, 45, 46, xii

Cornish Hush 1, 3, 5, 6, 7, 9, 10, 14, 15, 16, 17, 18, 23, 35, 38, 48, 49, 50, 63, 103, 104, 113, 119, xiv, xv

Crewe Works 29

Crich 117, 118

D Dot 34

Drawings

Engine shed for Samson 118

Lewin Guinness loco *(diagram)* 24

Little Grimsby *(side elev. only)* xiii

Little Nut 43

Rail section & chairs 17

Samson 110-111

Samson *(construction)*

Frames 52

Wheel centres 60

Cylinder 66

Crankshaft & supports 68

Motion work 74

Feed pump & reverser 84

Tender for Samson 115

E Eaton Hall 31

Ebbw Vale Steel,

Iron and Coal Company Ltd 30

Effie 30

Ella 30

G Geoghagan, Samuel 34

Groove Rake 38

Guinness Brewery 22, 23, 24, 25, 29, 30, 50, 104, xv

H Hawkwood Burn 6, 11, 12, 13, 14

Heywood, Sir Arthur 23, 29, 30, 31, 32, 82, 83

Hops 22, 23, 24, 25, 29, 33, 50, 78, 104

Horwich Works 23, 30, 33, 116

Howden Burn 1, 3, 6, 7, 9, 11,

Hude Top Fitting Shops 3

Hudswell Clarke 39

Hunslet 63

J John Fowler 27, 33, xii

K Katie 30, 31, 32, 82

Killhope 114

L Laxey Mine 26, 29

Lewin, Stephen ix, 20, 21, 22, 23, 25, 29, 30, 34, 44, 46, 48, 49, 50, 61, 78, 83, 86, 100, 103, 104, xiv, xv

Lindholme 25, 33

Little Dorrit 30

Little Grimsby 38, xiii

Little Nut 39, 40, 41, 42, 43, 50, 120

Little Sally 37, 38, 39, 120

LNWR 23, 28, 30

London Lead Company 1, 2, 3, 22, 38, 39, 41, 49, 50, 103, 104, 112, 113, xv

M Malt 22, 23, 24, 25, 29, 33, 50, 78, 104

Maps

Bollihope (geological) 6

Bollihope 1898 8

N Narrow Gauge Railway Museum 29, 34

Neilson 28

Nenthead 112, 113

No.1 - see 'Coffee Pot'

No.18 20, 22, 23, 48

P Pease, Edward 2

Pet 29,

Pinkney, Mark 3

R R & W Hawthorn 38, 39, 50

Ramsbottom, John 28, 29, 30

Rookhope 38, 39, 120

S SAMUK 3, 6, 9, 10, 38, 119

Severn Valley Railway 47, 53, 83, 98, xiv

Sharp, Stewart 29, 30, 34

Sir Vincent 27

Snowplough 42

Stanhopeburn 3, 37, 38, 39, 119, 120,

Statfold Barn 47, 59

Station Road Steam 31, 32

Steam Mule 47, 49, 98, xii

Stephen Lewin & Company

Stephenson, George 117,

Stephenson, valve gear 23, 33, 72, xii

T Tarrant, William 21, 22, 26, 27, 30

Tow Law 28

U Ursula 31, 32

V Vielle Montagne Company 3

W Waterfield, James 30, 32, 82

Weardale Lead Company 36, 38, 39, 42

Whitfield Brow 1, 3, 7, 9, 12, 14, 15, 16, 49

Wolfcleugh 37, 39, 120

Wren 33, 34, 48, 116

Y Young, David vii, ix, 20, 45, 116, xi